MIDDLE EASTERN DELICACIES
200 YEARS OF CULINARY HERITAGE

Traditional - healthy and vegetarian recipes

Written by
Nelly Sultan

and

Nina Mellman S.N.H. Dip (Nutrition)

Dedicated to my great grandfather
and my grandfather
for sharing all their knowledge

Tribute

Tribute to our family doctor in Egypt
Dr. Tewfik Ta'laat Bey
(Bey being the honorary title for services rendered to the state.)
(The title Bey is equivalent to Sir in English)

He was not only a Bey but a highly respected dignitary
with a noble and big heart.
He was more than a doctor of medicine, he was also a dietician and a hygienist of the
highest calibre. Medicine was his vocation. All the knowledge and principles gained at
university were enhanced by an inborn intuition and common sense.

In Egypt all frequent contagious diseases, such as typhoid, malaria etc., were treated at
home. It would have been very difficult to implement the treatments required to bring about
a full recovery, without the help, advice and daily visits of our doctor.

For example, typhoid fever required a very strict hygiene, care and re-hydrating diet regime
over a period of 3 to 4 weeks, all under his personal and constant surveillance.
As soon as the fever subsided, the first consistent meals were bean purée (see recipe for
foul medames purée) fortifying and full of minerals, as well as yoghurt (the probiotics it
contains are very important for strenghening the intestinal flora and the immune system)
and citrus sweet jelly (in those days it was fish gelatine).

For many diseases, in addition to medication a dietary regime is paramount in the therapy
for the return to full health.

Mother and daughter at the market

As mother and daughter we have co-operated to pass on our knowledge and 'know how' on the national dishes of our country of birth Egypt and that of our ancestors Syria and Lebanon.

Preface

My mother, born in 1922 in Heliopolis Egypt, came from a large family as with most of the families in those days. They were used to cooking on a grand scale and all the dishes, desserts, pastries, jams, pickled vegetables in jars, rose water and orange flower water, were all home made.

Her father and grandfather were herbalists and " apothecary " by profession in Aleppo Syria. Even in those days they had already adopted a healthy lifestyle and diet. All her life, my mother has been greatly influenced by the advice and remedies handed down to her by her father and grandfather.

As for me, I live in England and was for many years in the food industry, I used to devise recipes and produce ethnic foods based on my knowledge of Middle Eastern specialities for some of the major supermarkets in the UK.
Having studied, and obtained a Diploma in Nutrition, I joined forces with my mother to adapt our traditional family recipes.

A good light and healthy diet should not contain too much animal fat and too much sugar. Fat and sugar sap the energy required for digestion and elimination. They are the causes of many ailments. Even in their days, our grandparents, by reason of their profession, were already certain of these facts.
Just as Hippocrates used to say, food should be our first medicine.

All the recipes we share with you in this book come from family traditions handed down over the generations. We have lightened the traditional recipes following the principles of today's modern healthy diets, without compromising on all the flavours and aromas of old.

For all our meat filled specialities, we have created a vegetarian version rich in vegetable proteins of comparable taste. Vegetarians will not feel frustrated any more as they will finally be able to sample and appreciate our mediterranean and middle eastern specialities.

When one eats a delicious meal in France, it is customary to say "Que du bonheur" (what happiness), in Egypt they used to say "Ma cha Allah " meaning " what God would have wished for ".

In this book, we are bringing to you all the flavours of the exotic Middle East and the Ottoman empire, with traditional, as well as healthy and vegetarian recipes, lower in fat and sugar but high in flavours.
To all our readers, in true middle eastern hospitality " Et Fada Lou " you are welcome at our table.

Nina Mellman S.N.H. Dip. (Nutrition)

TABLE OF CONTENTS

Principles followed

Eggs
We advise organic or free range.

Fish
We advise line caught, wild or organic.

Flour
Unless otherwise stated
use plain white organic flour.

Garlic
Fried garlic is often indigestible. It should
be added raw in the cooking process in
order to retain its beneficial properties. We
recommend fresh garlic when in season
(April / May). When being used in hors
d'oeuvres, it should be blanched for a few
seconds (this will diminish its strong smell
and will render it more digestible).

Meat and poultry
We advise the use of organic or free range.

Milk / Cheese
These have all been retained in the
traditional recipes. For those who are
lactose intolerant, we have substituted
milk by soya milk, cream cheese by Labna
(see recipe), milk yoghurt by soya yoghurt
(without lactose and without cholesterol).

Oils
No hydrogenated oils have been used. We
recommend you use first cold pressed oils,
such as olive oil, rapeseed (canola), or any
other organic oil.
For cooking : olive oil or cold pressed
rapeseed should be used.
For frying : preferably use groundnut oil.
For pastries : we advise light olive oil, butter
or organic margarine.

Pepper, nutmeg, cumin, cinnamon, clove, etc.
Add a small amount at the start of the
cooking process and the rest at the end, in
order to obtain beautifully seasoned dishes.

Salt
We use natural sea salt and we always use
salt sparingly.
For green vegetables, add the salt at the
start of the cooking process.
For pulses, add salt at the end of the
cooking (salt slows the cooking process).

Soya
The soya mince also called textured
vegetable protein, is used in some of our
vegetarian recipes as a substitute to the
meat and chicken.

Sugar
We have used organic raw sugar and we
have often substituted sugar by honey. The
quanties have been kept to a minimum
wherever possible

Tofu
Soya bean curd pressed and formed
into blocks. It has the appearance of
cheese, with a neutral taste. Its versatility
enables it to absorb the flavours of other
ingredients. It can replace meat and dairy
for vegetarians and vegans.

For your information
The majority of the ingredients are available
from health food shops or from specialist
Middle Eastern (Greek, Lebanese) and
ethnic grocery stores. Some are also now
available in supermarkets.

Aromatic plants

The aromatic plants, dill, basil, chive, green coriander, marjoram, mint, oregano, parsley, rosemary, sage, thyme (za'atar), as with the condiments and spices, are used for their flavours as well as their medicinal properties.

They are best consumed fresh and green. When the leaves loose their vivid green colours and turn yellow they could become toxic such as yellowing parsley.

Spices and condiments

Middle Eastern cuisine would not have acquired its famous reputation without the use of all the fragrant spices and condiments.

The use of condiments and spices, has enabled many ethnic groups to add the appropriate complementing condiments to each dish. They have now become part of their customary diets.The condiments and spices were not added to the dishes uniquely for their flavours, but for their medicinal properties, digestive, antiseptic, etc.

Are best used in moderation.

Spices and condiments most commonly used in the Middle East

Béharat *

Citric acid **

Cinnamon

Cardamom

Coriander seeds

Coriander, fresh

Cumin

Cayenne pepper

Mahlab (powder extracted from cherry stones)

Mastic (sap from pistachio trees) ***

Nigella or black cumin seeds (Hab el Baraka) or black onion seeds

Panama bark (soapwort root)
(extract of tree bark from Brazil used for foaming effect)

Pomegranate molasses

Sahlab (powder of orchid bulbs)

Sumac (powder of dried berries)

Scented waters :

Orange flower water

Rose water

Tamarind (Indian date)

Turmeric

Za'atar (thyme flower)

* Beharat
Composition of spices, frangrant but not hot :
2 tbsp of these 4 spices (nutmeg, cinnamon, clove and pepper) or allspice
1 tbsp black pepper, 1 tbsp white pepper
1 tsp of rosebuds (optional)

** Citric acid can be found in a powder form and replaces lemon juice in some dishes

*** Mastic
The mastic is the resin from pistachio tree (Pistacia lentiscus), very aromatic it is used in small doses in Middle Eastern pastries and desserts, such as loukoums (turkish delights) and ice creams.
Just like the scented flower waters it gives an exotic perfume and flavour typical of the Middle East. For use and our original recipe of mastic with sugar see page 249.

4 National Dishes of Egypt

Foul medames (small dried brown beans)
Red lentil soup
Molokheya soup (green corchorus leaves or lalo)
Ta'ameya / Falafel (rissoles of beans or chick peas)

4 National Dishes of Syria-Lebanon

Kibbeh / Kobeba
Stuffed vine leaves
Lahm be adjin (small meat pizza)
Koftas with meat

Hors d'Oeuvres – Mezzes

Artichoke Salad (raw)

PREPARATION 30MIN
INGREDIENTS (SERVES 4)
- **4** Artichokes, fresh (small like violets, poivrade)
or frozen artichoke bottoms or hearts
- **1** Garlic clove blanched and mashed
- **2** tbsp Lemon juice
- **1** tbsp Olive oil
- **1** pinch Salt

METHOD

1 Peel the artichokes, discard the choke and the stalk, wash and retain the bottoms or the hearts (if tender).

2 Finely slice the artichokes bottoms, if using the small hearts keep them whole, if they are large cut them in two or quarters.

3 Season with garlic, lemon, oil, salt and mix thoroughly.

SUGGESTION

Marinate for 30 min. to allow the seasoning
to impregnate and the flavours to develop.
When eating raw garlic it is advisable to blanch it first,
this removes it's strong taste whilst retaining it's flavour.
(Blanching : Immerse the garlic clove in boiling water for 1 to 2 min)

Aubergine baba ganoush
Aubergine dip

PREPARATION 20 MIN
COOKING 15 MIN

INGREDIENTS (SERVES 4)

- **1** Aubergine (400 g. approx.)
- **1** Garlic clove (blanched and mashed)
- **1** Bunch of parsley (chopped)
- **1** tbsp Tahini paste
- **1** tbsp Oil
- **1** tbsp Lemon juice
- **1** pinch Salt

METHOD

1 Dilute the tahini paste in two tablespoons of water and set aside.
2 Wash the aubergine.
3 Place the aubergine on a preheated griddle and turn it frequently.
4 As soon as it is well grilled, allow to cool, then remove the skin.
5 Mash the aubergine with a fork, add the tahini, garlic, parsley, oil, lemon juice and salt. Taste and adjust the seasoning if required.

ADVICE

When eating raw garlic it is advisable to blanche it first, this removes it's strong taste whilst retaining it's flavour.
(Blanching: immerse the garlic in boiling water for 1 to 2 minutes)

Doa and Za'atar Seasoning

These blends of exotic spices used as seasoning, are well appreciated for their flavours as well as for their health properties.
They were the poor man's meal, due to the cheap ingredients used.
You could season a large round pitta bread with a tablespoon of doa or za'atar.
The doa is an egyptian speciality and the za'atar a lebanese and syrian speciality.

The doa as they say in Arabic : "bet ched el alb"
meaning it reinvigorates the heart and is an instant "pick me up",
due to the strong aroma emanating from the roasted spices.

My mother's snack at school
During her childhood in Egypt, my mother's snack used to consist
of half a pitta bread with some labna and doa or za'atar (thyme - see recipe)
with slices of cucumber.
Some children not familiar with this aromatic kind of sandwich,
tempted by the appetising aroma, often used to ask if she would be
willing to exchange her snack for theirs.

Doa

PREPARATION 60 MIN

INGREDIENTS
- 100 g Whole sesame seeds
- 20 g Coriander seeds
- 1 tsp Cumin powder
- ½ tsp Salt

METHOD

1 Sort the sesame and coriander seeds
in order to remove any impurities (twigs or stones).
2 Gently toast in a frying pan separately,
the coriander seeds then the sesame seeds.
3 Allow to cool, then finely grind in a coffee grinder separately,
the coriander and the sesame.
Mix the ground coriander and ground sesame with the cumin and salt,
then grind again. You should aim for a fine texture.

ADVICE

Be careful not to over toast the ingredients as you risk burning
their oils and could render the mix indigestible.
Place in an airtight container. Keeps a long time in the fridge.

SUGGESTION

The doa is eaten sprinkled over pitta bread, toast or crackers spread with
butter, labna or feta cheese topped with cucumber slices.
It can also be enjoyed mixed with natural yoghurt.
In Egypt the doa used to be eaten sprinkled over a large sesame seed bagel
shaped bread called sémite, which used to be sold by street vendors shouting
" doa, sémite, taza ! " taza meaning at the peak of freshness.

Za'atar

Thyme

PREPARATION 15 MIN
INGREDIENTS

- 50 g Za'atar powder (thyme)
- 20 g Sesame seeds lightly toasted
- 1 pinch Citric acid or ½ tsp sumac
- 1 pinch Salt

METHOD

In a bowl mix all the ingredients thoroughly.

ADVICE

This mix of za'atar may also be purchased
in ethnic and middle eastern grocers.
Store in a hermetically sealed jar.

SUGGESTION

Usually served as a mezze with olive oil
or sprinkled over labna (see recipe) or salads.
Mixed with olive oil may be used as a middle eastern
substitute for italian pesto.

RECOMMENDATION

Citric acid and sumac may be found in ethnic grocers.

Filo - Spinach borek
Spinach triangles

PREPARATION 40 MIN
COOKING 25 MIN
INGREDIENTS (18 PIECES)
- 6 sheets Filo pastry (40cm x 30cm approx)
- 70 ml Oil
- 1 tbsp Sesame seeds (for sprinkling)

FILLING
- 80 g Frozen chopped spinach
- 1 Onion finely chopped (35 to 45 g)
- 30 g Grated cheese, cheddar, gruyère, feta or other (or mashed tofu)
- 1 Egg beaten (save 1 tbsp for glazing)
- 20 g Breadcrumbs
- 1 tbsp Oil
- 1 pinch Salt
- 1 pinch Pepper
- 1 pinch Nutmeg (optional)

METHOD - FILLING

1 Put the oil in a frying pan, add the chopped onion and cook over low heat until softened and translucent, add the frozen spinach. Cook for approximately 10 min until all the water has evaporated.

2 Add the grated cheese (or tofu mashed with a fork), the egg, breadcrumbs, salt, pepper and nutmeg (if used), mix together thoroughly and set aside.

METHOD - ASSEMBLY

1 Take 6 sheets of filo pastry together. On the 40 cm side cut 3 equal lengths of 13 cm x 30 cm approx. which will give 3 strips per sheet (Fig. 1). Keep all the strips in a plastic bag in order to stop them drying.

2 Take one of the pastry strips and brush it with oil (Fig. 2), fold it in two lengthways and brush it with oil again (Fig. 3)

3 Place one heaped teaspoon of filling the size of a walnut diagonally at the beginning of the strip (Fig. 4) and fold over to form a triangle with regular sides. Fold the triangle over itself tightening the filling with the filo pastry whilst folding over (Fig. 5, 6, 7), till the sheet of pastry ends as a triangle (Fig. 8). Proceed in the same manner with all the other strips.

4. Place all the boreks on a lined baking tray. Brush with oil, the reserved beaten egg, then sprinkle with sesame seeds (see Fig. 8, 9)

5 Place in a preheated oven at 175 º C. (gas mark 3 1/2) for 10 to 15 min. Prior to taking them out, check the pastry is a light golden brown.

ADVICE
This size is ideal for a mezze buffet.
You can make them larger if you wish.

RECOMMENDATION
Filo pastry is available in most supermarkets and ethnic stores.

Filo - cheese Borek

Cheese Triangles

PREPARATION 40 MIN BAKING 15 MIN
INGREDIENTS (18 PIECES)

- 6 sheets Filo pastry (40cm x 30cm approx.)
- 70 ml Oil
- 1 tbsp Sesame seeds (for sprinkling)

FILLING

- 40 g Tofu or a boiled potato mashed with a fork
- 60 g Grated cheese, cheddar, gruyère, feta or other (or tofu)
- 1 tbsp Grated parmesan
- 1 Egg beaten (save 1 tbsp for glazing)
- 1 pinch Salt
- 1 pinch Pepper
- 1 pinch Nutmeg (optional)

METHOD - FILLING

In a bowl, mix the tofu or the potato, the cheese,
egg, salt, pepper and nutmeg if used.

METHOD - ASSEMBLY

See recipe filo- spinach borek.

ADVICE

This size is ideal for a mezze buffet. You can make them larger if you wish.

RECOMMENDATION

Filo pastry is available in most supermarkets and ethnic stores.

Filo - meat Borek
Traditional meat Triangles

PREPARATION 40 MIN COOKING 20 MIN
INGREDIENTS (18 PIECES)

- 6 sheets Filo pastry (40cm x 30cm approx.)
- 70 ml Oil
- 1 tbsp Sesame seeds (for sprinkling)

FILLING

- 120 g Minced meat
- 1 Onion chopped (60 to 70 g)
- 2 tsp Pomegranate molasses or lemon juice
- 1 tsp Tomato purée (concentrate)
- 2 tbsp Oil
- 2 tbsp Water
- 1 pinch Salt
- 1 pinch Pepper béharat or black pepper with a pinch of allspice
- 15 g Pine nuts (optional)
- 20 g Pomegranate seeds (optional)

METHOD - FILLING

1 Put the chopped onion in a bowl add the minced meat and mix thoroughly.

2 Put the 2 tablespoons of oil in a frying pan, then add the onion and meat mix.
Stir over a moderate heat for 5 min. Add the water, molasses, tomato purée, salt and pepper .

METHOD - ASSEMBLY
See filo - spinach borek. For glazing, you may substitute some milk or soya milk for the egg.

NOTE
Filo pastry is available in most supermarkets and ethnic stores.

Filo - vegetarian Borek
Vegetarian triangles

PREPARATION 40 MIN COOKING 25 MIN

INGREDIENTS (18 PIECES)
- 6 sheets Filo (40cm x 30cm approx.)
- 70 ml Oil
- 1 tbsp Sesame seeds (for sprinkling)

FILLING
- 25 g Tofu
- 1 Onion chopped (40 to 50 g)
- 30 g Soja mince (fine textured vegetable protein)
- 3 tbsp Oil
- 2 tsp Pomegranate molasses or lemon juice
- 1 tsp Tomato purée (concentrate)
- 100 ml Water
- 1 pinch Salt
- 1 pinch Béharate pepper or black pepper with a pinch of allspice
- 20 g Pine nuts (optional)
- 20 g Pomegranate seeds (optional)

METHOD - FILLING

1 Put the 3 tablespoons of oil in a frying pan, add the onion and cook over low heat until softened and transluscent.

2 Add the water, the tofu mashed with a fork, soya mince, tomato purée, pomegranate molasses, salt and pepper. Cook whilst stirring until complete evaporation of the water. Add the pine nuts and the pomegranate seeds if used and set aside.

METHOD - ASSEMBLY

See recipe filo - spinach borek. For glazing, you may substitute some milk or soya milk in place of an egg.

ADVICE

This size is ideal for a mezze buffet. You can make them larger if you wish. They are as tasty as the meat boreks. Vegetarians will not feel frustrated any more and will be able to enjoy this speciality.

RECOMMENDATION

Filo pastry is available in most supermarkets and ethnic stores.

Filo - spinach Roll

PREPARATION 40 MIN COOKING 30 MIN
INGREDIENTS 1 ROLL (SERVES 4)
- 2 sheets Filo pastry (40cm x 30cm approx.)
- 4 tbsp Oil or butter or 2 tbsp oil and 2 tbsp butter
- 1 tbsp Sesame seeds (for sprinkling)

FILLING
- 45 g Chopped frozen spinach
- 1 Onion chopped (30 to 40 g)
- 2 tbsp Oil
- 35 g Grated cheese, cheddar, gruyère, parmesan, feta or tofu mashed with a fork
- 1 tbsp Breadcrumbs (10 g approx.)
- 1 Egg beaten (reserve 2 tbsp for glazing)
- 1 pinch Salt
- 1 pinch Pepper
- 1 pinch Nutmeg (optional)

METHOD - FILLING

1 Put the 2 tablespoons of oil into a frying pan, add the chopped onion
and cook over low heat for 5 min. until softened and transluscent.

2 Add the frozen spinach and the salt. Cover and cook over moderate heat
until complete evaporation of the water.

3 In a bowl mix the egg, spinach, cheese, breadcrumbs, salt, pepper and nutmeg if used, then set aside.

METHOD - ASSEMBLY

1 Place a sheet of filo flat over a work surface and brush it lightly with oil Fig.1.

2 Place the second sheet directly on top and brush it with oil Fig.1.

3 Fold both sheets together over 10 cm approx. in the 40 cm length, brush with oil Fig. 2 ,
place the spinach mix over the folded strip leaving 3 cm clear from each end Fig. 3.

4 To hold the filling in place, fold over the two edges at the sides and brush them with oil. Fig. 4.

5 Fold the filo pastry tightly over the spinach and roll to form a roll of 5 cm wide Fig. 5. As you first start to
roll, brush the whole length of the filo with oil, continue rolling and keep brushing at every turn Fig. 6.

6 Transfer the roll on a lined baking tray, brush the top with oil and the reserved egg, sprinkle with sesame
seeds Fig. 7. Place in the preheated oven at 175 ° C (gas mark 3 1/2) for 15 to 20 min.
Prior to taking them out, check the pastry is a light golden brown.

ADVICE

You can mix the cheeses for a more subtle taste. If you are only using tofu
you should add a little more salt, pepper and nutmeg to enhance the flavour.

RECOMMENDATION

The filo pastry is available in most supermarkets or ethnic stores.

Kahk
Savoury Sesame Seed Rings

PREPARATION 30 MIN PAUSE 1H BAKING 20 MIN
INGREDIENTS (30 PIECES)

- 235 g Flour, plain white (fine)
- 80 ml Oil
- 90 ml Water
- 9 g Dried yeast
- 1 tsp Aniseeds (optional)
- 1 tsp Black onion seeds (hab el baraka, black cumin seeds) (optional)
- ½ tsp Mahlab powder (cherry stone extract), (optional)
- ½ tsp Salt

FOR DECORATION

- 1 Egg beaten with a pinch of salt
- 40 g Sesame seeds

METHOD - PASTRY

1 In a bowl mix the flour, yeast, aniseeds, black onion seeds, oil and salt.

2 Add the water a little at a time, draw all the ingredients together and start kneading until complete absorption of the water. The dough should be firm but not too soft.

3 Cover with a cloth or cling film and leave to rise for 1 hour.

METHOD - FORMING THE KAHK AND BAKING

1 Weigh the dough and divide it in 30 equal parts of 12 to 13 g approximately.

2 Take one part, form it into a ball, then roll it into a little stick of 13 to 14 cm long and shape it into a ring Fig. 1, 2, 3.

3 Put the beaten egg in a saucer, add a pinch of salt and put the sesame seeds in another saucer.

4 Dip the ring first in the egg then in the sesame seeds Fig. 4, 5. Place it on a lined baking tray Fig. 6 and proceed in the same manner with the rest of the dough.

5 Bake in a preheated oven at 180ºC (gas mark 4) for 15 to 20 min. approx.

6 Remove from the oven as soon as they are golden brown. Allow them to cool slightly, then taste. If the Kahks are not crunchy, place the tray back into the hot switched off oven for a further10 min.

ADVICE

The kahks can be stored in an airtight container for a long time.
Once cooked they may be frozen.
After 5 min of taking out of the freezer, the kahks may be eaten and will still be crunchy.

RECOMMENDATION

All the spices are available in ethnic stores specialising in middle eastern produce.

Kibbeh/Kobeba
Filled Bulgar Dough

**MIDDLE EASTERN PEOPLE'S FAVOURITE DISH
HAS PRIDE OF PLACE AT ALL PARTY BUFFETS
NO "MEZZES" WITHOUT KIBBEHS**

This dish requires both dexterity and patience.
For speed and ease to form the tubes, a special adaptor is available as an
attachment to an electric or hand mincer. One can then obtain fine
and regular long tubes that can be cut to the desired length.

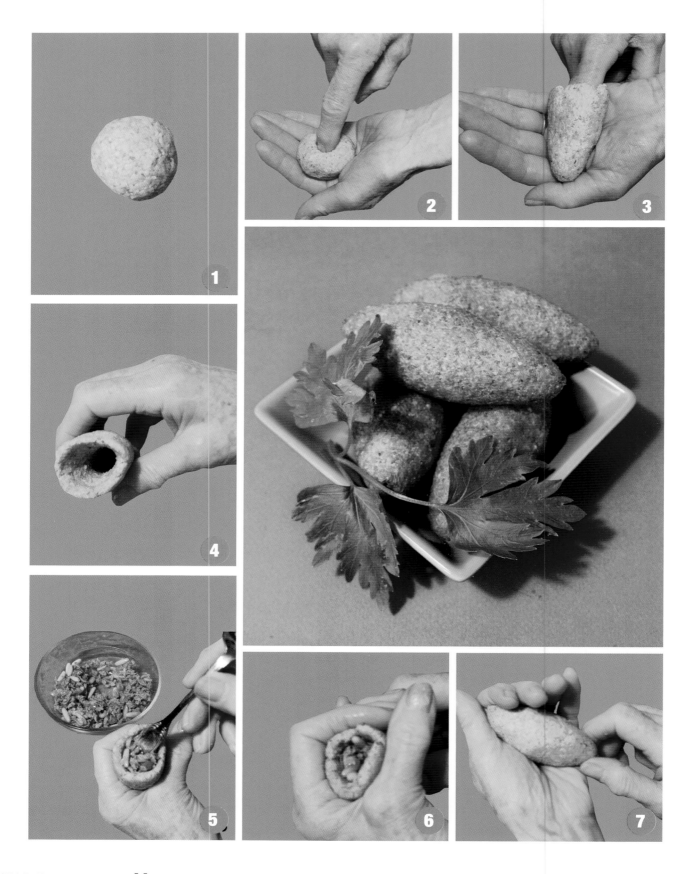

Kibbeh/Kobeba with meat
Traditional meat filled bulgar dough

PREPARATION 1H 30 COOKING 30 MIN (COOKING AND FRYING)
INGREDIENTS (12 PIECES)

BULGAR DOUGH TUBES
- 180 g Bulgar wheat (fine)
- 100 g Flour, plain white
- 100 ml Water (for soaking)
- 1 tsp Cumin powder
- 3 tbsp Oil
- 80 ml Water
- 1tsp Salt

FILLING
- 100 g Minced meat
- 1 Onion, chopped (150 g approx.)
- 2 tbsp Oil
- 1 tsp Tomato purée (concentrate)
- 2 tsp Pomegranate molasses
  (or 2 tsp lemon juice)
- 3 tbsp Water
- 1 pinch Salt
- 1 pinch Pepper béharat or black pepper with
  a pinch of allspice
- 20 g Pine nuts
- 20 g Pomegranate seeds (optional)
- 50 cl Oil for frying (groundnut oil preferably)

METHOD - DOUGH TUBES
1 Wash the bulgar wheat in a sieve.
2 Soak the washed bulgar wheat in a bowl in the 100 ml of water for 15 min.
3 Add the flour, cumin, oil, salt, the 80 ml of water and mix thoroughly.
Allow to rest for 15 min.

METHOD - FILLING
1 Mix the minced meat with the chopped onion.
2 Put the oil in a frying pan, add the onion and meat mix and stir fry for 2 to 3 min. over a moderate heat. Add all the other ingredients except the pepper, the pine nuts and the pomegranate seeds. Mix well and leave to cook uncovered until complete evaporation of the water. Add the pepper, the pine nuts, the pomegranate seeds (if used) and set aside.

METHOD - ASSEMBLY
1 Fill a small bowl with a little water for moistening your hands as required.
2 Take a piece of bulgar dough (50 g approx.). Dampen your hands, then squeeze the dough to soften it while kneading it in between the palms of your hands to form a ball Fig. 1.
3 Whilst holding the ball in the palm of one hand, use the dampened index finger of the other hand to bore a hole in the centre. Continue turning the dough around the index finger to form a hollow cylindric tube of 8 to 10 cm long and 3 cm in diameter (approx.) without piercing the bottom Fig. 2, 3, 4.
4 Using a teaspoon fill the tube with the filling compacting it well to the bottom with the spoon handle, stopping 1 cm from the top Fig. 5.
Should the dough crack whilst working, dip a finger in water and smooth over the crack to seal it. To close the tube squeeze the top whilst
continually turning to seal it well Fig. 6.
5 Ensure the two ends are identically shaped Fig. 7.
6 Deep fry in groundnut oil preferably.

ADVICE Whilst the bulgar wheat is soaking, prepare the filling. The kibbehs need to be deep fried in the same manner as french fries, allow 500 ml of oil, the volume of oil relates to the size of your fryer. To test the oil temperature, put a piece of bread in the hot oil, as soon as it is golden brown the oil is at the correct temperature.
Deep fry in small batches in order to maintain the oil temperature.

SUGGESTION These Kibbehs are best eaten with tahini sauce. They may be frozen raw. These Kibbehs require «know how» and a certain agility of the hands. For ease and speed see the recipe for «Kibbeh in a Tray».

Kibbeh/Kobeba vegetarian
Filled bulgar dough

**PREPARATION 1H30 COOKING 30 MIN. (COOKING AND FRYING)
INGREDIENTS (12 PIECES)**

BULGAR DOUGH TUBES
- 180 g Bulgar wheat (fine)
- 100 g Flour, plain white
- 100 ml Water (for soaking)
- 1 tsp Cumin powder
- 3 tbsp Oil
- 80 ml Water
- 1 tsp Salt

FILLING
- 30 g Soya mince (textured vegetable protein) fine
- 1 Onion chopped (100 to 150 g)
- 2 tsp Pomegranate molasses or 2 tsp lemon juice
- 1 tsp Tomato purée (concentrate)
- 3 tbsp Oil
- 150 ml Water
- 1 pinch Salt
- 1 pinch Pepper béharat or black pepper with a pinch of allspice
- 20 g Pine nuts
- 20 g Pomegranate seeds (optional)

METHOD - DOUGH TUBES
See preceding recipe for kibbeh with meat.

METHOD - FILLING
1 Put the 3 tablespoons of oil in a frying pan, cook the chopped onion
over a moderate heat for 5 min until softened and transluscent.
2 Add the water and all the other ingredients except for the pine nuts
and the pomegranate seeds. Allow to cook covered over a low heat for 10 min.
3 Uncover and stir until complete evaporation of the water.
Switch off, add the pine nuts, the pomegranate seeds (if used) and set aside.

METHOD - ASSEMBLY
See preceding recipe for kibbeh with meat.

*These meat tasting kibbehs will finally
allow vegetarians to appreciate this speciality.*

Kibbeh/Kobeba bel saneya with meat
Traditional Kibbeh on a tray

PREPARATION 40 MIN
COOKING 50 MIN.
INGREDIENTS (SERVES 4)
DOUGH
- 100 g Bulgar wheat (fine)
- 50 g Flour, plain white
- 50 ml Water (for soaking)
- 2 tbsp Oil
- 1 tsp Cumin powder
- 1 tsp Salt
- 3 tbsp Water

MEAT FILLING
- 100g Minced meat
- 1 Onion chopped (100 g approx.)
- 2 tbsp Oil
- 2 tsp Pomegranate molasses or 1 tsp lemon juice
- 1 tsp Tomato purée (concentrate)
- 3 tbsp Water
- 1 pinch Salt
- 1 pinch Pepper béharat or black pepper with a pinch of allspice
- 20 g Pine nuts
- 20 g Pomegranate seeds (optional)
- 3 tbsp Oil (for drizzling over the top)
- 1 tbsp Sesame seeds (for sprinkling on top)
- 1 Ovenproof dish 19 cm x 14 cm approx.

METHOD - DOUGH
1 Wash the bulgar wheat in a sieve.
2 Soak the washed bulgar wheat in a bowl in the 50 ml of water for 15 min.
3 Add the flour, cumin, oil, salt, the 3 tablespoons of water and mix well. Set aside for15 min.

METHOD - FILLING
1 Put the minced meat and chopped onion in a bowl and mix thoroughly.
2 Put the 2 tablespoons of oil in a frying pan, add the meat and onion mix. Stir fry over moderate heat for 2 to 3 min. Add the 3 tbsp of water, tomato purée, pomegranate molasses, salt and pepper. Allow to cook uncovered whilst stirring until the complete evaporation of the water.
3 Add the pine nuts, the pomegranate seeds (if used) and set aside.

METHOD - ASSEMBLY
1 Put half the bulgar dough in an ovenproof dish lined with baking parchment and pack well down using the back of a spoon.
2 Put the filling over the dough and again press and pack well down.
3 Put the other half of the bulgar dough on top and press all 3 layers down again.
4 Drizzle the 3 tbsp of oil over the dough and sprinkle with the sesame seeds.
5 Place in a preheated oven at 180 ° C (gas mark 4) for 35 to 40 min.

ADVICE
Whilst the bulgar wheat is soaking, prepare the filling.
Unlike the filled kibbeh (traditional individual ones) this kibbeh recipe is much easier and quicker to prepare without any frying.
SUGGESTION
Can be eaten with tahini sauce and a middle eastern salad as an accompaniment.

Kibbeh/Kobeba
bel saneya vegetarian
Kibbeh on a tray

PREPARATION 40 MIN
COOKING AND OVEN TIME 50 MIN
INGREDIENTS (SERVES 4)

DOUGH
- 100 g Bulgar wheat (fine)
- 50 g Flour, plain white
- 50 ml Water (for soaking)
- 2 tbsp Oil
- 1 tsp Cumin powder
- 1 tsp Salt
- 3 tbsp Water

FILLING
- 50 g Soya mince (fine)
- 1 Onion chopped (100 g approx.)
- 3 tbsp Oil
- 2 tsp Pomegranate molasses
or 1 tsp lemon juice
- 1 tsp Tomato purée (concentrate)
- 250 ml Water
- 1 pinch Salt
- 1 pinch Pepper béharat or black pepper
with a pinch of allspice
- 20 g Pine nuts
- 20 g Pomegranate seeds (optional)
- 3 tbsp Oil (for drizzling)
- 1 tbsp Sesame seeds (for sprinkling)
- 1 Ovenproof dish 19 cm x 14 cm
(approx.)

METHOD - DOUGH
1 Wash the bulgar wheat in a sieve.
2 Soak the washed bulgar wheat in a bowl
in the 50 ml of water for 15 min.
3 Add the flour, cumin, oil, salt,
the 3 tablespoons of water and mix well.
Allow to rest for 15 min.

METHOD - FILLING
1 Put the 2 tablespoons of oil in
a frying pan over a moderate heat,
add the chopped onion and cook for 5 min
until softened and translucent.
2 Add the water, soya mince, molasses,
tomato purée, salt and pepper. Cover and cook
over moderate heat for 10 min approximately.
3 Uncover and stir until complete
evaporation of the water. Take off the heat,
add the pine nuts and the pomegranate
seeds if used and set aside.

METHOD - ASSEMBLY
See preceding recipe for
Kibbeh bel saneya with meat

Labna (Yoghurt curd cheese)
Milk or soya milk yoghurt speciality

INGREDIENTS
• 500 g Plain live yoghurt or soya live yoghurt (organic)
•1 tbsp Olive oil
•1 pinch Salt

METHOD
1 Pour the yoghurt in a sieve lined with a muslin cloth (or any fine white cloth) tie the four corners of the muslin together and leave to drain
overnight.
2 The next day upturn the resulting moulded curd cheese
over a bowl and peel the cloth away. Add the salt and olive oil,
mix well and adjust the seasoning to your taste.

ADVICE
Kept in the refrigerator, it will keep for over a week.
For those intolerant to milk, the labna made with live soya yoghurt easily replaces cream cheese and is a good substitute for creme fraiche and dairy cream, without lactose, rennet and cholesterol.
Suitable for vegetarians and vegans.
Low in calories, high in vegetable protein and probiotics.

SUGGESTION
You can season it with za'atar (thyme), doa or dried mint.
Makes a wonderful herb cream cheese substitute,
with the addition of garlic and herbs.
Can be eaten with salt, or sweetened with fruit coulis as a dessert.

ORIGINAL RECIPE
Traditionally the labna was made with cow's, sheep or goat' s milk
yoghurt. It was shaped into balls the size of walnuts and kept in olive oil in a
sealed jar.

Lahm be adjin with meat
Traditionnal recipe (Meat pizza)

PREPARATION 60 MIN
PAUSE 50 MIN BAKING 15 MIN
INGREDIENTS (12 PIECES)

DOUGH
- 250 g Flour, plain white
- 21 g Fresh yeast or 9 g dried yeast
- 2 tbsp Oil
- 1 pinch Salt
- 200 ml Water (tepid)

FILLING
- 200 g Minced meat
- 1 Onion chopped (100 g approx.)
- 2 tbsp Pomegranate molasses or
1 tbsp of lemon juice
- 1tbsp Tomato purée (concentrate)
- 1 pinch Salt
- 1 pinch Pepper béharat or pepper with a
pinch of allspice
- 20 g Pine nuts (optional)
- 30 g Sesame seeds (optional)

METHOD - DOUGH
1 Dissolve the yeast in 50 ml of tepid water
(taken from the 200 ml).
2 In a bowl, mix the flour salt and oil. Add the
yeast mixed in water. Bring all the
ingredients together by hand to form a ball.Start
kneading whilst adding the rest of the water little
by little to form a soft and malleable dough. Cover
with a cloth and leave to rise for 50 min.

METHOD - FILLING
Put the minced meat in a bowl, add the chopped
onion, tomato purée, pomegranate molasses or
lemon juice, salt and pepper. Amalgamate all the
ingredients, add half the pomegranate seeds and
half the pine nuts if used, mix well and set aside.

METHOD - ASSEMBLY AND BAKING
1 Weigh the whole dough and divide it into
12 equal parts of 30 g each approximately. Form
into balls and set aside Fig. 1, 2.
2 Place a ball onto a lightly floured work
surface and flatten it with your hand or with a
rolling pin to form a circle of 10 cm in diameter
approximately Fig. 3.
3 Put 1 tbsp of filling in the middle Fig. 4.
4 Spread the filling by patting it gently so it
adheres to the dough Fig. 5, 6. forming a lahm be
adjin. Proceed in the same manner for the rest of
the dough balls.
5 Place the lahm be adjins on to a lined baking
tray. Bake in the preheated oven at 180 ° C (gas
mark 4) for 15 min. approximately.
After baking decorate with the remainder of the
pomegranate seeds and the pine nuts.

ADVICE
Do not add the whole quantity of water all at once,
as depending on the quality of the flour the dough
may require a little less or more water.

SUGGESTIONS
Serve with tahini sauce and a middle eastern
salad (see recipe).
For cocktails you can make smaller dough bases.

Lahm be adjin vegetarian
Vegetarian pizza

**PREPARATION 60 MIN PAUSE 50 MIN
BAKING 15 MIN
INGREDIENTS (12 PIECES)**

DOUGH

- 250 g Flour, plain white
- 21 g Fresh yeast or 9 g dried yeast
- 2 tbsp Oil
- 1 pinch Salt
- 200 ml Water

FILLING

- 50 g Tofu
- 30 g Soya mince
(textured vegetable protein) fine
- 1 Onion, chopped (150 g approx.)
- 4 tbsp Oil
- 2 tbsp Pomegranate molasses or lemon juice
- 1 tbsp Tomato purée (concentrate)
- 200 ml Water
- 1 pinch Salt
- 1 pinch Pepper béharat
or black pepper with a pinch of allspice.
- 20 g Pine nuts (optional)
- 30 g Pomegranate seeds (optional)

METHOD - DOUGH

See preceding recipe for Lahm be Adjin
with meat.

METHOD - FILLING

1 Put the 4 tbsp of oil in a frying pan over a moderate heat till softened and transluscent.
2 Add the water, the tofu mashed with a fork,
soya mince, pomegranate molasses, tomato purée, salt and pepper. Mix it all thoroughly, cover
and cook for 10 min.
3 Uncover and stir until complete
evaporation of the water. Adjust the
 seasoning to your taste.
Take off the heat and add half the
pomegranate seeds and half the pine nuts if used,
mix well and set aside

METHOD - ASSEMBLY AND BAKING

See preceding recipe for Lahm be adjin with
meat.

ADVICE

Do not add the whole quantity of water all at
once, as depending on the quality of the flour the
dough may require a little less or more water.

SUGGESTIONS

Serve with tahini sauce and a middle eastern
salad (see recipe).
For cocktails you can make smaller dough bases.

ORIGINAL RECIPE

Used to be made only with meat.

Samboussek with cheese
Cheese turnover (shortcrust pastry)

PREPARATION 50 MIN

BAKING 20 MIN

INGREDIENTS (20 PIECES)

DOUGH
- 200 g Flour, plain white
- 100 ml Oil
- 50 ml Water
- 1 pinch Salt
- 1 tbsp Sesame seeds (for decoration)

FILLING
- 60 g Cheese, grated cheddar, gruyere, comté, or any other cheese
- 20 g Parmesan cheese, grated
- 1 Egg, beaten (reserve 2 tbsp for glazing)

METHOD - DOUGH
Put the flour, salt, oil and water in a bowl, draw all the ingredients together to form a ball, then start kneading until you obtain a malleable dough.

METHOD - FILLING
Put the cheeses in a bowl, mix with the beaten egg and set aside.

METHOD FOR ASSEMBLY
1 Weigh the dough and divide it in 12 parts of 28 g each approximately. Shape each part into a ball and set aside Fig. 1.
2 In order to stop the dough sticking to the rolling pin or the work top, take a piece of grease proof paper, fold it in two put a dough ball inside. Flatten it with the rolling pin, forming a circle of 10 cm in diameter approximately Fig. 2.
3 Put a teaspoon of the cheese mix in the centre of the circle and fold the circle in two Fig. 3, 4.
4 Press the edges together and trim the surplus dough with an upturned glass to form a sealed turnover (samboussek) Fig. 5, 6.
5 Retrieve the surplus of dough from each samboussek to form 8 more dough balls.
6 Place the sambousseks on a lined oven tray, brush with the reserved egg and sprinkle with the sesame seeds Fig. 7.
7 Bake in a preheated oven at 180 ° C (gas mark 4) for 15 to 20 min. Remove when nicely golden.

ADVICE
Do not add the whole quantity of water all at once, as depending on the quality of the flour the dough may require a little less or more water. May be frozen raw.

ORIGINAL RECIPE
Used to only be made with butter.

Samboussek with meat
Meat turnover / traditionnal recipe

PREPARATION 50 MIN
COOKING 25 MIN
INGREDIENTS (15 PIECES)

DOUGH
- 190 g Flour, plain white
- 50 ml Oil
- 80 ml Water
- 1 pinch Salt

FILLING
- 120 g Minced meat
- 1 Chopped onion (70 g approx.)
- 1 tsp Pomegranate molasses or lemon juice
- 1tsp Tomato purée (concentrate)
- 1tbsp Oil
- 3 tbsp Water
- ½ tsp Salt
- 1 pinch Pepper béharat
or black pepper with a pinch of allspice
- 15 g Pine nuts (optional)
- 25 g Pomegranate seeds (optional)
- 350 ml Oil for frying

METHOD - DOUGH
Mix the flour, salt and oil in a bowl, add the water and draw all the ingredients together to form a ball, then start kneading for 5 min. until you obtain a malleable dough.

METHOD - FILLING
1 In a food processor, mix the chopped onion, the minced meat, the tomato purée, the pomegranate molasses and the salt.
2 Lightly warm 1 tablespoon of oil in a frying pan over a medium heat, add the meat mix and stir fry for 2 to 3 min.. Add the 2 tablespoons of water, cover and allow to cook for 5 min.
3 Uncover the pan and stir until the complete absorption of the water. Add the pepper, the pine nuts and the pomegranate seeds if used and set aside.

METHOD - ASSEMBLY
1 Weigh the dough and divide it in 15 parts of 20 g each approximately. Form each part into a ball and set aside.
2 In order to stop the dough sticking to the rolling pin or the work top, take a sheet of grease proof paper, fold it in two put a ball of dough inside. Flatten it with a rolling pin to form a circle of 10 cm in diameter Fig.1, 2.
3 Put a tablespoon of filling in the centre and fold the circle in two to form a samboussek Fig. 3, 4.
4 Close the edges by pressing the dough 1 cm from the edge, make festoons or crimp with a fork at 1 cm of the edge in order to stop the filling oozing out during the frying Fig. 5, 6, 7. Proceed in the same manner with the other dough balls.

FRYING
Put the oil to heat in a frying pan. To test if the oil has reached the correct temperature put a samboussek in and keep turning it at regular interval until golden brown. Remove it with a slotted spoon. Fry the rest in small batches at a time. Take care as they fry very quickly. When taken out of the fryer, lay them over absorbant kitchen paper.

ADVICE
Do not add the whole quantity of water all at once, as depending on the quality of the flour the dough may require a little less or more water.

SUGGESTION
Best eaten hot with a middle eastern salad and tahini sauce.

Samboussek with vegetarian filling
Vegetarian turnover

PREPARATION 50 MIN COOKING 30 MIN
INGREDIENTS (15 PIECES)

DOUGH
- 190 g Flour, plain white
- 50 ml Oil
- 80 ml Water
- 1pinch Salt

FILLING
- 25 g Tofu
- 30 g Soya mince (textured vegetable protein) fine
- 1 Onion, chopped (50 to 60 g approx.)
- 2 tbsp Oil

- 1tsp Tomato purée (concentrate)
- 1tsp Pomegranate molasses or lemon juice
- 150 ml Water
- 1 pinch Salt
- 1 pinch Pepper beharat or black pepper with a pinch of allspice
- 20 g Pine nuts (optional)
- 20 g Pomegranate seeds (optional)
- 350 ml Oil for frying

METHOD - FILLING

1 Put the 2 tablespoons of oil in a frying pan over a medium heat, add the chopped onion and stir till softened and transluscent.
2 Add the water, the tofu mashed with a fork, soya mince, tomato purée, pomegranate molasses (or lemon juice) salt and pepper.
Mix thoroughly, cover and cook over a medium heat for 10 min.
3 Uncover and stir until the complete evaporation of the water.
At the end of the cooking, adjust the seasoning to your taste, take off the heat, add the pine nuts and the pomegranate seeds (if used) and set aside.

METHOD - DOUGH AND FRYING

See preceding recipe for Samboussek with meat.

Falafel / Ta'ameya
Chick peas rissoles

PREPARATION 30 MIN
COOKING 40 MIN
INGREDIENTS
(20 PIECES APPROX.)

- 150 g Chick peas soaked overnight or black beans (foul medames) soaked and peeled
- 400 ml Water
- 1 bunch Coriander, fresh (20 g approx. or 2 tbsp of frozen coriander)
- 1 bunch Parsley, flat variety (20 g approx.)
- 1 Onion (60 g approx.)
- 2 Garlic cloves
- ½ tsp Coriander powder
- ½ tsp Cumin powder
- 20 g Cornflour
- 1 tsp Baking powder
- 20 g Breadcrumbs
- 1 tbsp Oil
- 50 ml Water (taken from the cooking water)
- 1 tsp Salt
- 1 pinch Cayenne pepper (optional)
- 400 ml Oil for frying

METHOD

1 Cook the chick peas in the 400 ml of water for 20 min.
2 Drain the chick peas and retain the water.
3 In a food processor or a mincer, finely mince together the chick peas, parsley, coriander, onion and garlic, add the rest of the ingredients with 50 ml of water taken from the cooking water.
Mix well to amalgamate all the ingredients to obtain a sticky mixture. Let the mix rest for an hour.
4 Dampen your hands, then take a tablespoonful of the mixture the size of a walnut (20 g approx.), with the palms of your hands, squeeze it and roll it into a ball then flatten it to form a rissole of approximately 5 cm in diameter.
5 Put the oil to heat in a pan, as soon as the oil is hot, fry the falafels till they are a nice golden brown.
Remove and place on absorbent kitchen paper to drain.

ADVICE

If an electric fryer with thermostat is not available, for all frying here is a good tip : Put a small piece of bread to fry In the hot oil (groundnut preferably), as soon as it is golden brown you can fry the falafels. If the oil is not at the right temperature the falafels could desintegrate.
If you are using the peeled small black beans (foul medammes) proceed in the same manner as for the chick peas.

SUGGESTIONS

The falafels may be served on their own as a mezze or can be eaten as a sandwich in a pitta bread pocket with oriental salad and tahini sauce. As a variation they may be shaped into little balls of 10 g approx. May be frozen raw or fried.

ORIGINAL RECIPE

Were only made with brown beans (foul medammes).
The beans used to be sprouted by soaking 3 or 4 days in water then peeled prior to using. The falafels were also made by mincing the beans (foul medames) or the chick peas raw. The cooking process renders them more digestible.

THE SALADS

On our arrival in France in 1950, whenever we ordered salads in restaurants,
to our astonishment we were served with
a few lettuce leaves seasoned with vinegar.
We used to reflect « is this what they call a salad ?».
It used to be eaten at the end of the meal, which we found surprising as our
salads were part of our hors d'oeuvre or used to
accompany our main courses.
For us a salad always comprises of several vegetables and herbs, seasoned
with olive oil, lemon juice and salt.

We recommend you eat it at the beginning of a meal.
It is more beneficial for the digestion and the figure.

Salads

Middle eastern salad

PREPARATION 30 MIN
INGREDIENTS (SERVES 4)

- ½ Cucumber or 1 small cucumber
- 2 Tomatoes
- 1 Red onion or spring onion or a few sprigs of chives
- 2 Sprigs of mint, leaves finely chopped
- 1 Bunch of parsley (flat variety), finely chopped
- 2 tbsp Olive oil
- 1 tsp Lemon juice
- 1 pinch Salt

METHOD

1 Dice the cucumber, tomatoes and onion, place in a bowl,
add the mint, parsley, salt, lemon juice and oil.

2 Mix well, taste and adjust the seasoning if required.

3 Let it rest for 10 min before serving.

ADVICE

Leaving the salad to rest will allow the vegetables to absorb the seasoning.
This salad is the basis for the Fattouche and the Tabouleh salads (see recipes).

Fattouche salad
Salad with bread

PREPARATION 30 MIN
INGREDIENTS (SERVES 4)
- 1 Middle eastern salad (see preceding recipe)
- 50 to 60 g Stale bread
- ½ tsp Sumac (optional)
- 30 ml Water

METHOD

1 Wet the stale bread with the 30 ml of water.

2 Squeeze it in your hands to remove the excess water.

3 Cut it in small pieces and mix with the middle eastern salad.

Add the sumac (if used), taste and adjust the seasoning if required.

A good way to use up leftover bread.

Tabouleh
Bulgar wheat salad

PREPARATION 40 MIN
INGREDIENTS (SERVES 4)

- 1 Middle eastern salad (see recipe)
- 60 g Bulgar wheat (fine)
- 30 ml Water (for soaking)

METHOD

1 Wash the bulgar wheat in a sieve, put it in a bowl, add the 30 ml of water and let it soak for 30 min.
2 Squeeze the bulgar wheat with your hands to remove the excess water, if necessary. The grains should be soft, swollen and separate.
3 Add to the middle eastern salad and adjust the seasoning to your taste.

Tahini dip
Sesame Seeds paste

PREPARATION 20 MIN
INGREDIENTS (SERVES 4)
- 3 tbsp Tahini paste concentrate
- 1 Garlic clove blanched and crushed
- 3 tbsp Lemon juice
- 6 tbsp Water
- ½ tsp Cumin powder
- ½ tsp Salt
- 1 bunch Parsley (flat variety), finely chopped

METHOD

1 Blanch the garlic by boiling it for 2 min in 3 tablespoons
of water (taken from the 6 tablespoons of water).
Take the garlic clove out and save the water. Crush the garlic clove and set aside.
2 Put the tahini paste in a small bowl, add the lemon juice, salt, cumin, the blanched
and crushed garlic, the 3 tablespoons of water remaining in
addition to the garlic water saved for creaming the tahini paste.
3 Mix thoroughly to obtain a smooth and homogenised cream, if necessary add more
water for the desired consistency. Taste and if required adjust the seasoning, then mix
in the parsley reserving 1 teaspoon for sprinkling over the top.

ADVICE

When eating raw garlic it is advisable to blanch it first, this removes it's strong taste
whilst keeping it's flavour.
The tahini paste is sold as a concentrate to be diluted and seasoned. Mix well before
using as the sesame oil tends to separate and migrate to the top.

SUGGESTION

The tahini sauce is eaten with the foul medames,
the kibbehs, or as a "dip" for crudités

Yoghurt with cucumber and mint (tsatsiki)

PREPARATION 15 MIN
INGREDIENTS (SERVES 4)

- 4 Small pots of 125 g of milk or soya yoghurt
- 100 g Cucumber
- 1 Garlic clove (blanched) or ½ teaspoon of garlic powder
- 1 tsp Dried mint
- 2 tbsp Water
- 1 pinch Salt
- 8 leaves Fresh mint to decorate

METHOD

1 Blanch the garlic by boiling it in 2 tablespoons of water for 2 min in order to lessen its strong taste. Keep the water from the blanched garlic for the seasoning.
2 Empty the yoghurt pots into a mixing bowl, add the 2 tablespoons of water plus the water left from the blanched garlic, the dried mint, the blanched and crushed garlic clove and the salt. Mix all the ingredients thoroughly.
3 Add the washed, unpeeled (if organic) and diced cucumber.
Serve in 4 little bowls and decorate with the fresh mint leaves.

SUGGESTION

When eating raw garlic it is advisable to blanch it first, this removes it's strong taste whilst keeping it's flavour.
Serve with ice cubes, ideal as a starter for summer meals.

BREAD IN EGYPT

We still remember the good and tasty wholemeal bread with bran which used to be called
"Pain Baladi" (poor people's bread) with a fine texture
and a very crispy crust.
White bread was the preserve of the rich !
Nowadays it is the opposite, wholemeal flour is dearer than
white flour.
Why make your own bread when you can so readily buy baked bread everywhere.
Unfortunately, there is no comparison.
We have often been tempted to buy the commercially made breads, but as we read the list
of ingredients we were astounded of all the preservatives, flour improvers, raising agents,
hydrogenated vegetable fats and others, etc.
However, the only ingredients required to make good bread are a good flour, fresh yeast
and water.

Breads

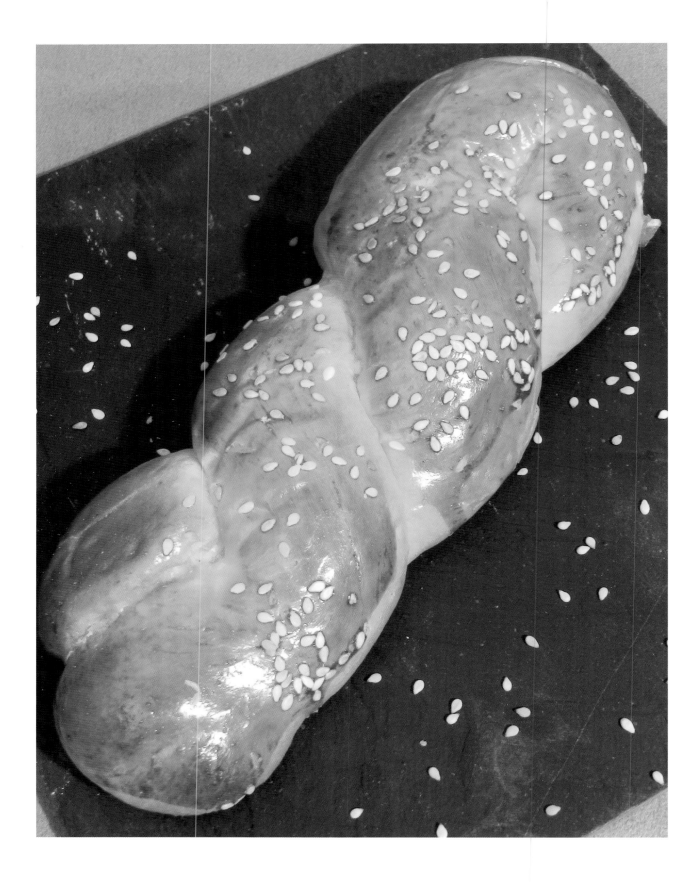

Chorek
Platted Brioche style bread

PREPARATION 25 MIN PAUSE 3 H 30 MIN BAKING 20 MIN
INGREDIENTS (2 LOAVES)

- 300 g Flour, plain white
- ½ pack Fresh yeast (21 g) or dried yeast (9 g)
- 1 Egg beaten (reserve 1 tbsp for glazing the loaves)
- 20 g Sugar
- 50 ml Oil
- 120 ml Water (tepid)
- 1 pinch Salt
- ½ tsp Mahlab (optional see condiments)
- 10 g Sesame seeds for sprinkling

METHOD

1 In a bowl dilute the yeast in a little tepid water taken from the 120 ml,
add the beaten egg, the sugar and mix well.

2 Put the flour, salt and oil in a mixing bowl and blend together.
Add the mix of yeast egg and sugar. Stir while drawing all the ingredients together.
Add the rest of the water a little at a time while kneading until complete absorption
of the water and the dough becomes soft and malleable.

3 Cover with a cloth and leave to rise for 3 hours.

4 Form 6 balls of dough of equal size.

5 Roll each ball into sausage shapes of 25 cm long approximately.
Place 3 sausage shaped lengths side by side, press together the 3 ends at one end only, platt
and finish by pressing well together the other 3 ends so the platted dough does not come undone
whilst cooking. You have now shaped the first loaf.
Repeat the process with the other 3 lengths of dough to form the second loaf.

6 Lay the 2 loaves on a lined oven tray, cover with a cloth and leave to rise for another 30 min.
Uncover and brush the loaves with the reserved beaten egg, then sprinkle the sesame seeds.

7 Bake in the preheated oven at 180 ° C (gas mark 4) for 15 to 20 min until golden brown.

ADVICE

Do not add the whole quantity of water all at once, as depending
on the quality of the flour the dough may require a little less or more water.

SUGGESTIONS

You can add raisins and also make some small round buns.
Once baked the loaves may be frozen.

Baladi bread
Pitta bread with bran

PREPARATION 30 MIN PAUSE 1 H 15 MIN
BAKING 10 MIN
INGREDIENTS (14 PIECES)

- 250 g Flour, plain strong
- 20 g Wheat bran
- ½ pack Fresh yeast (21 g) or dried yeast (9 g)
- 1 tbsp Oil
- 200 ml Water (tepid)
- 1 tsp Sugar
- 1 pinch Salt

METHOD

1 Dilute the yeast in a little tepid water taken from the 200 ml.

2 Mix the flour, salt and oil in a mixing bowl then add the diluted yeast.
Mix well drawing all the ingredients together, then knead whilst adding the water a little at a time till you obtain a soft and malleable dough.
Cover with a cloth and let it rest and prove for 1 hour.

3 Weigh the whole dough and divide it in 14 parts of 30 g each approximately.
Roll each part into a ball and set aside.

4 On a worktop dusted with wheat bran, place a dough ball and flatten it,
dust bran over the top. With the rolling pin shape into rounds of 10 cm in diameter.

5 On a lined oven tray, lay and space the shaped breads,
to allow them to swell and rise. Let the breads rest for another 15 min.

6 Heat the oven to 180 ° C (gas mark 4) for 15 min.
Switch off the oven and switch on the grill.
Put the tray in the oven under a medium grill for 5 to 10 min leaving
the door ajar the whole time, this method allows the bread to rise and swell.

7 As soon as the breads are out of the oven,
cover them with a clean cloth to stop them going hard.

ADVICE

Do not add the whole quantity of water all at once, as depending
on the quality of the flour the dough may require a little less or more water.

Pitta bread

PREPARATION 30 MIN PAUSE 1 HR 15 MIN
BAKING 10 MIN
INGREDIENTS (14 PIECES)
- 250 g Flour, plain white
- ½ pack Fresh yeast (21 g) or dried yeast (9 g)
- 1 tbsp Oil
- 200 ml Water
- 1 tsp Sugar
- 1 pinch Salt

METHOD
1 Dilute the yeast in a little tepid water taken from the 200 ml.
2 Mix the flour in a bowl with the salt, the sugar and the oil. Add the diluted yeast while drawing all the ingredients together and knead whilst adding the water a little at a time to obtain a soft and malleable dough. Cover with a clean cloth and let the dough rise for 1 hour.
3 Weigh the whole dough and divide it into14 equal parts of 30 g each approximately.
Roll into balls and flatten each ball by hand or with a rolling pin
to shape round breads of 8 cm in diameter approximately.
4 On a lined baking tray place and space all the breads to allow
for swelling and rising. Allow to rise for a further 15 min.
5 Heat the oven at 180 ° C (gas mark 4) for15 min. Switch off the oven and switch
on the grill. Place the tray under a medium to hot grill with the oven door ajar for 5 to 10 min.
This method allows the breads to rise and swell.
Remove from the oven when the breads are puffed and slightly golden.
6 As soon as the tray is out of the oven, cover it with a clean cloth to stop the breads going hard.

ADVICE
Do not add the whole quantity of water all at once, as depending on the quality of the flour the dough may require a little less or more water. A good idea for spreading the soft dough and stop it sticking to the worktop and the rolling pin, is to place a dough ball in between two pieces of greaseproof paper and shape it to your needs.

SUGGESTIONS
The pitta bread can be eaten as a sandwich. Make a slit to form a pocket, fill it with falafels (ta'ameya) or foul medammes with middle eastern salad and tahini sauce.
These are the traditional hot take away sandwiches sold in the Middle East, just like hamburgers are in the west. In half a pitta bread spread a little labna, sprinkle some doa or za'atar and a few slices of cucumber. They were the tasty snacks of our childhood.

Semite
Bagel shaped bread with sesame seeds

PREPARATION 30 MIN
PAUSE 3 HR 30 MIN BAKING 20 MIN
INGREDIENTS (3 PIECES)

- 300 g Flour, plain white
- ½ pack Fresh yeast (21 g) or dried yeast (9 g)
- 1 tbsp Oil
- 1 Beaten egg (reserve 1 tbsp for glazing)
- 150 ml Water (tepid)
- 20 g Sugar
- 1 pinch Salt
- 25 g Sesame seeds (for sprinkling)

METHOD

1 Dilute the yeast in a little tepid water taken from the 150 ml. Add the sugar, the beaten egg and mix well.

2 Put the flour with the salt in a mixing bowl, add the oil. Add the yeast egg and sugar mix, draw all the ingredients together and knead whilst adding the rest of the water a little at a time to form a soft and malleable dough.
Cover with a clean cloth and allow to rise for 3 hours.

3 Form 3 sausage shaped lengths of equal weight of 50 cm long approximately, join the 2 ends of every length to form a ring (a semite).
Proceed in the same manner with the other 2 lengths to form 2 more semites.

4 Lay the semites over a lined baking tray and allow to rise for another ½ hour.

5 Brush the top with the reserved beaten egg, sprinkle with the sesame seeds and put in a preheated oven at 180 ° C (gas mark 4) for 15 to 20 min until the semites are a golden colour.

ADVICE

Do not add the whole quantity of water all at once, as depending on the quality of the flour the dough may require a little less or more water.

SUGGESTIONS

The semite is eaten with doa, za'atar, cheese or hard boiled eggs.

In Egypt, the semite was often sold by street merchants shouting '
' Semite taza, guebna, bede ! " translated means " fresh semite, cheese,
hard boiled egg ! " It was enjoyed any time of the day.

SOUPS

In order to obtain meat or chicken based soups without any fat, we recommend you cook the meat or chicken stocks the day before, place in the refrigerator and the next day skim the stock to remove all the fat that has migrated to the surface.

Soups

Foul nabet
Sprouted brown beans soup

PREPARATION 30 MIN COOKING 40 MIN
INGREDIENTS (SERVES 4)
- 200 g Little brown beans (egyptian beans " foul medammes")
- 1 Onion (50 to 60 g) quartered
- 3 Garlic cloves (whole)
- 1 pinch Turmeric
- 1 tbsp Oil
- 1 L (1000 ml) Water

After cooking
- 3 tbsp Lemon juice
- 1 tbsp Oil
- 1 tbsp Cornflour (diluted in 4 tbsp of water)
- ½ tsp Sugar (optional)
- ½tsp Salt

METHOD

Soak the beans 2 to 3 days while changing the water daily, so they can sprout a little.
Peel the beans once they have sprouted.
1 Put the litre of water in a large casserole with the peeled beans, onion, garlic and the turmeric. Bring to the boil, lower the heat and simmer covered for 30 min. Allow to cool.
2 Purée the beans using an electric hand blender, liquidiser or a food processor.
3 Reheat gently then add the oil, lemon, salt, sugar (if used) and the diluted cornflour then bring to the boil uncovered while stirring for 10 min allowing the cornflour to cook and thicken.
Before switching off the heat, check and adjust the seasoning to your taste.

ADVICE

To save time, in ethnic stores you can purchase the dried beans already peeled.
The same as with all pulses you only need to soak them overnight and cook them the next day. However the taste and the health benefits do not compare with that of freshly sprouted beans.

SUGGESTIONS

While serving, garnish each plate with fresh coriander, parsley, chives etc.

ORIGINAL RECIPE

This soup is fortifying and full of minerals. It used to be given to convalescents.

Ham'd with aubergines
Aubergine and lemon soup

PREPARATION 15 MIN COOKING 25 MIN
INGREDIENTS (SERVES 4)

- 2 Aubergines (450 to 500g) peeled and diced
- 5 Garlic cloves crushed
- 1 tbsp Dried mint
- 4 tbsp Lemon juice
- 2 tbsp Oil
- 200 ml Pomegranate juice fresh or bottled (optional)
- 1.25 L (1250 ml) Water or chicken / meat stock
- 1 Tamarind pod or 1 tsp of sugar (optional)
- 1 tsp Salt

METHOD

1 Put the water or stock (chicken or meat) in a large casserole, add the washed, peeled and diced aubergine with the pomegranate juice (optional), the lemon juice, mint, crushed garlic, oil, tamarind pod or sugar (if used) and salt. Bring gently to the boil, lower the heat, cover and simmer for 25 min.

2 As soon as the aubergines are cooked, before taking off the heat, taste and adjust the seasoning to your taste.

ADVICE

When buying aubergines, they should be firm and jet black, shiny and light in weight (which means it will have less pips). Try and add the pomegranate juice as it will enhance the flavour. Nowadays the benefits of pomegranates are much lauded.
To extract the juice from the pomegranate, cut it in 2 and use a lemon squeezer.
For health reasons tamarind pods are more beneficial than sugar.
Break the pod, remove the stone and retain the paste.

SUGGESTION

To be served with rice, it was inconceivable to enjoy this soup without 2 to 3 tablespoons of rice. "Ham'd" in Arabic means acidic.

Ham'd with celery and potatoes

Lemon, celery and potato soup

PREPARATION 30 MIN COOKING 30 MIN
INGREDIENTS (SERVES 6)

- 150 g Celery stalks (ribs)
- 200 g Celeriac
- 150 g Parsnips or replace with potatoes or celery
- 200 g Potatoes
- 4 Garlic cloves crushed
- 5 tbsp Lemon juice
- ½ tsp Turmeric
- 1.3 L (1300 ml) Water or stock chicken / meat
- 2 tbsp Oil
- 1 tsp Salt

METHOD

1 Put the washed celery cut up in chunks into a large casserole with the peeled and diced celeriac, potatoes and parsnips (if used).
Add garlic, lemon juice, water or stock (chicken / meat), turmeric and salt.
2 Bring to the boil, lower the heat, cover and simmer for 30 min.
Check the seasoning and adjust to your taste.

ADVICE

This soup is served with rice and as an option with the rice Kibbehs
(see following recipe). If you serve this soup with the rice kibbehs, add them when the soup starts to boil, to allow them to cook with the vegetables.

ORIGINAL RECIPE

It used to be cooked with potatoes and celery only.
The addition to this recipe of the celeriac and the parsnips has greatly enriched the soup's content with vegetables and enhanced its flavour.
The garlic was always fried.

Ham'd with celery and rice kibbeh / kobeba

Stuffed rice dumpling with meat or tofu

PREPARATION 40 MIN
COOKING 30 MIN
INGREDIENTS (15 PIECES)

SOUP Ham'd with celery
and potatoes (see preceding recipe)

DOUGH
- 70 g Ground rice or rice for grinding
- 55 g Oat bran
- 65 g Minced meat or 50 g tofu, mashed
- 1 Egg
- 1 tbsp Oil
- 1 tbsp Water
- 1 pinch Salt
- 1 pinch Pepper

FILLING
- 30 g Minced meat or tofu, mashed
- 30 g Celery stalks (ribs)
- 1 tbsp Oil
- 1 pinch Salt
- 1 pinch Pepper

FOR ASSEMBLING
- 1 tbsp Oil
- 1 tbsp Water

METHOD - DOUGH

1 To make your own ground rice, wash the rice the day before use, let it dry, then pulverise in a grinder, or use some ready made ground rice.
2 Mix the meat or the tofu with the ground rice and oat bran, add the beaten egg, oil, pepper and salt. Amalgamate it all well in a food processor and set aside.

METHOD - FILLING

Mix the meat or the tofu, with the celery cut up into small chunks, add the oil, season and set aside.

METHOD - ASSEMBLY

1 Put the oil and water in a saucer and wet your palms.
2 Form dough balls of rice of 15 g approx.
3 Take a ball in the palm of one hand, with the slightly wet index finger of the other hand bore a hole in the centre whilst
continually turning the dough ball around your finger, at the same time applying
pressure to the palm of your hand in order to strech the pastry and obtain the hollowed shape of an emptied egg shell.
4 Introduce 1teaspoon of filling, pack down gently using the handle of the spoon. To close the top, squeeze the end while continually turning. Shape both ends identically forming a rice kibbeh. Proceed in the same manner for the remaining rice balls.
5 As soon as the Ham'd soup is boiling, put the kibbehs to cook with the vegetables for 30 min.

ADVICE

You will find ground rice and oat bran in some supermarkets or health food shops.
For the shaping of the kibbehs see illustrated method for meat kibbehs page 44.

SUGGESTION

Serve one or two kibbehs per soup bowl.The rice kibbehs can also be added to a vegetable soup. May be frozen raw if the meat has not been previously frozen.

ORIGINAL RECIPE

These rice kibbehs were always made with meat and had a very compact texture. The addition of the oat bran lightens the texture.

Lentil soup

PREPARATION 20 MIN COOKING 30 MIN
INGREDIENTS (SERVES 6)

- 150 g Lentils (red split lentils)
- 150 g Carrots
- 150 g Pumpkin or replace with carrots
- 1 Onion (100 g approx.)
- 2 Garlic cloves
- ½ tsp Turmeric
- 2 tsbp Oil
- 800 ml Water

Seasoning at the end of the cooking
- 600 ml Water
- 1 tsp Cumin powder
- 1 tsbp Cornflour (diluted in 4 tbsp of water)
- 2 tsbp Oil
- 4 tsbp Lemon juice
- 1 tsp Salt

METHOD

1 Sort the lentils to remove any impurities, wash and drain.

2 Put the washed carrots and the peeled pumpkin cut up in chunks in a large casserole. Add the lentils, the peeled onion, garlic, turmeric, water, oil. Bring gently to the boil uncovered as the lentils foam and risk spilling over. As soon as the foam has subsided, lower the heat, cover and allow to simmer for 20 min.

3 Remove from the heat, allow to cool uncovered for 10 min.

4 Purée the soup in a blender, food processor or electric hand held blender.

5 Replace over the heat, add the 600 ml of water, cumin, oil, lemon juice, salt, the diluted cornflour, bring to the boil uncovered for 10 min whilst stirring. Check the seasoning and adjust to your taste.

ADVICE

If you buy organic carrots, you will only need to scrub them before use. If you use a hand held blender, you can purée the soup in the casserole, saving time and extra handling.

SUGGESTION

It may be served garnished with chopped chive, chopped fresh coriander and croutons.

ORIGINAL RECIPE

Used to be made without turmeric, carrots, pumpkin and onion only with the "ta'aleya" (garlic and dried coriander fried). For a healthier alternative we have now removed the ta'aleya.

In Egypt the red lentils were the poor man's meal eaten with the flat crusty oat bran bread (Baladi bread, see recipe page 81) and a salty raw onion.

This soup is a vitamin cocktail, full of beta carotene, rich in protein and slow absorbing carbohydrate (low glycemic).

Lentils well known as the dish for which in the Bible "Esau" sold his birthright !

MOLOKHEYA
(Green Corchorus leaves, Lalo for africans)

One of the most popular national soup of Egypt.
If one had to define only one egyptian dish it would be the molokheya.
With a very special taste and aroma. The main ingredients, especially
the coriander and the garlic give it a special fragrance and taste.

One either loves it or hates it.
Just goes to say, once tasted and liked this soup is irresistible.
If Esaü sold his birth right for a dish of lentils, the Egyptian would sell
his soul for a dish of molokheya.

Molokheya
Green Soup

PREPARATION 10 MIN COOKING 25 MIN
INGREDIENTS (SERVES 6)

- 400 g Molokheya frozen (1 pack)
- Fresh green coriander, small bunch chopped small
- 2 tbsp Coriander seeds grilled and ground (3 g approx.)
- 4 Garlic cloves crushed
- 1 Onion finely chopped (50 to 60 g)
- 2 tsbp Oil
- 1.75 L (1750 ml) Water or stock meat / chicken
- 1tsp Salt
- 1 pinch Pepper

METHOD

1 Put the water or stock in a large casserole, add the garlic, onion,
the 2 corianders, salt and pepper. Bring to the boil, lower the heat and simmer covered for 15 min.

2 Add the oil, the pack of frozen molokheya and stir to dissolve completely.

3 Allow to cook gently, uncovered (as it could spill over)
for another 10 min. Switch off the heat and cover.

4 Stir well before serving.

ADVICE

Sift through the coriander seeds and remove any impurities. Toast them lightly in a frying pan over a low heat to enhance the flavour. When cool grind them and keep in a sealed jar.
We don't advise the use of ready ground coriander as the flavour is different.
The grilling of the coriander, avoids frying it.
If available you can replace the frozen pack with 500 g of fresh leaves chopped in an electric mincer.
Although the frozen one is quicker and is still very tasty.

ORIGINAL RECIPE

The molokheya used to be made with fresh leaves, hand chopped with a mezzaluna
(in italian), demi lune (in french) (a semi circle knife).
It used to be made using chicken wings or meat ribs or other cuts of meat suitable for soup or with chicken stock.
Of course it used to be made with the traditional " ta'aleya " (garlic and ground coriander fried) which used to be added at the end of the cooking, the molokheya used to become heavy to digest and the smell of the ta'aleya used to waft into the whole neighbourhood. For a healthier version we have used the same ingredients without frying whilst retaining the original flavour.

Rechta
Soup with Pasta and Green or Black Lentils

PREPARATION 10 MIN COOKING 45 MIN
INGREDIENTS (SERVES 4)

- 120 g Lentils green / black
- 50 g Pasta (shells or flat noodles)
- 2 tbsp Oil
- 2 Garlic cloves crushed
- 1 tsp Coriander seeds (dried) grilled and ground
- 1 tbsp Fresh green coriander, chopped or frozen coriander
- 1.4 L (1400 ml) Water
- ½ tsp Salt

METHOD

1 Sort the lentils for any impurities, wash and drain.
Put the water in a large casserole, the lentils, the 2 corianders (fresh and dried),
the crushed garlic and the oil. Bring to the boil,
lower the heat cover and simmer for approximately 40 min.
Check the cooking, add the salt and the pasta, leave to boil for 5 min.
Before removing off the heat, check the seasoning and adjust to your taste.
2 Allow to rest for 15 min before serving.

SUGGESTION

Serve with a little fresh chopped coriander as a garnish.

ORIGINAL RECIPE

This soup used to be made with the ta'aleya (garlic and dried coriander fried)
added at the end of the cooking process. The association of the lentils
and the pasta makes this soup a complete vegetarian protein meal.

Vegetable Soup with vermicelli

PREPARATION 20 MIN COOKING 45 MIN

INGREDIENTS (SERVES 6)

- 2 Carrots
- 2 Leeks
- 2 Celery stalks (ribs)
- 1 Courgette
- 20 g Vermicelli
- 2 tbsp Oil
- 1.5 L (1500 ml) Water or stock of meat or chicken
- 1 tsp Salt

METHOD

1 Lightly grill the vermicelli in a frying pan over a medium heat, till pale gold. Take off the heat and set aside.

2 Put the water or the stock in a large casserole, add the oil, the leeks and the celery washed and cut up into small pieces, the carrots washed and thinly sliced. Cover and bring to the boil, reduce the heat and simmer for 20 min.

3 Add the courgette washed and sliced, allow to cook for another 10 min.

4 Switch off the heat, add the vermicelli, cover and leave for 15 min to allow the vermicelli to steam cook, prior to serving.

ADVICE

We lightly grill the vermicelli in a frying pan to keep it firm in the soup and stop it swelling and absorbing all the stock.

You can replace the vermicelli with little pasta tubes or any other pasta.

If the carrots and the courgette are large, cut them in two lengthways, before slicing.

MAIN COURSES

*In the Middle East main courses often evolved
around vegetables and pulses.
The vegetables were sautéed or simmered in a well seasoned
sauce with a few pieces of chicken or meat.
Vegetables were also filled with well seasoned meat and rice
and served as a main course with rice.*

*In Egypt we used to consume much more vegetables
and pulses than animal protein.
Small portions of meat and chicken,
were an accompaniment to the vegetables.
Nowadays we seem to have had a reversal,
the tendency is towards more meat , chicken etc.
and a few vegetables and pulses.*

*These days for a healthy diet, dietiticians
advise a return to the "old days"
when meat was a luxury. Now they recommend plenty
of vegetables and pulses, with less animal proteins.*

ARTICHOKE TALE

*As a child, I thoroughly disliked the artichoke.
My mother used to say to me : " It is a very healthy vegetable
and one should make the most of it while it is in season " not
appreciating it's health benefits and what a delicate gourmet dish
artichokes hearts are, very cross that I was made to eat them, my
answer always used to be
" This artichoke season is never ending !!! "*

*I must confess, now I adore fresh artichokes simmered
in chicken stock. What a joy !*

*" The king of vegetables " its benefits makes it an important
ally of the liver and the kidneys.*

Main courses

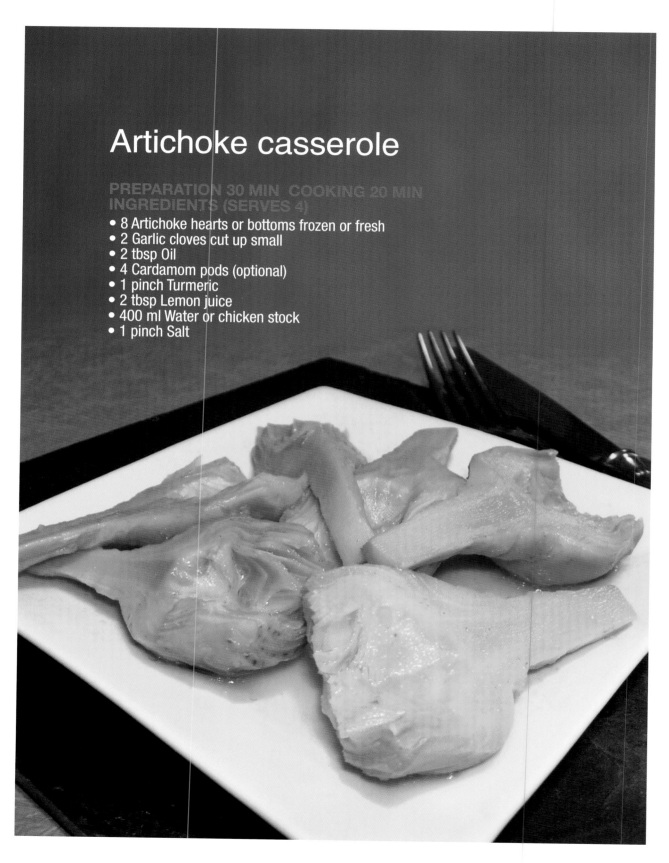

Artichoke casserole

PREPARATION 30 MIN COOKING 20 MIN
INGREDIENTS (SERVES 4)

- 8 Artichoke hearts or bottoms frozen or fresh
- 2 Garlic cloves cut up small
- 2 tbsp Oil
- 4 Cardamom pods (optional)
- 1 pinch Turmeric
- 2 tbsp Lemon juice
- 400 ml Water or chicken stock
- 1 pinch Salt

METHOD

1 Peel the artichoke until you expose the heart
(the middle) keeping a few of the soft leaves.
2 Cut up each artichoke heart in 4 and scoop out
the fibrous choke with a teaspoon.
3 Immerse the artichokes in water with lemon juice
to stop any discolouration.
4 Put the water or stock in a large casserole, add the garlic, oil, cardamom pods (if used), turmeric, lemon and salt. Bring to
boiling point, add the drained artichokes, cover and simmer for 20 min.

ADVICE

Peeling artichokes requires a certain know how, the use of frozen
artichokes hearts or bottoms, saves the arduous task of peeling. You would only
need to scold them first then proceed as with fresh artichokes.
If you are using fresh artichokes, we recommend the artichokes
"violet" (with a violet hue) or the small and elongated ones
"poivrade" (meaning in the shape of peppers).

ORIGINAL RECIPE

The fresh "violet" artichokes were always used.

Artichokes filled
with meat / chicken / tofu

PREPARATION 60 MIN
COOKING 40 MIN
(FRYING AND COOKING)
INGREDIENTS (SERVES 6)
- 12 Little artichoke bottoms
frozen (380 g approx.)

FILLING
- 100 g Minced meat or minced chicken
  breast or tofu mashed with a fork
- 3 tbsp Breadcrumbs
- 1 Egg
- 1 pinch Salt
- 1 pinch Pepper

SAUCE
- 400 ml Water or stock meat / chicken
- 2 Garlic cloves cut up small
- 2 tbsp Lemon Juice
- 3 Cardamom pods (optional)
- 1 pinch Turmeric
- 1 pinch Salt
- 1 pinch Pepper

COATING
- 1 Egg, beaten
- 100 ml Oil (for frying)

METHOD
Blanch the frozen artichoke bottoms
for 5 min, drain and set aside.

FILLING
Put the minced meat, or the minced chicken or
the tofu in a mixing bowl, add the breadcrumbs,
egg, salt, pepper and mix thoroughly. Fill the
artichokes bottoms with the filling, pack well
down delicately, taking care not to break them,
then set aside.

SAUCE
Put all the sauce ingredients in a large
casserole over moderate heat, bring to the boil
for 10 min and set aside.

COOKING
Heat the oil in a frying pan, dip the filled sides
of the artichokes in the beaten egg, then fry
lightly on both sides starting with the filled side
first. Place all the fried
artichokes in the casserole with the sauce,
filled side up. Cover and simmer on a low heat
for 30 min. Check the seasoning and adjust to
your taste.

ORIGINAL RECIPE
It was always made only with meat and with
fresh artichokes. The tofu version is an innova-
tion for vegetarians.

Aubergines with meat filling
Traditional Recipe

PREPARATION 30 MIN
COOKING 1 H
INGREDIENTS (SERVES 4)
- 8 Aubergines, small and long
(600 g approx.) black or white or
4 Larges aubergines sliced in 2
- 3 tbsp Oil
- 400 ml Water
- 1 Garlic clove, crushed
- 1 tsp Pomegranate molasses or lemon juice
- 1 pinch Salt
- 1 pinch Pepper
- 1 pinch Sugar (optional)

FILLING
- 150 g Minced meat
- 40 g Rice
- 1 tbsp Oil
- 100 ml Water
- 2 Garlic cloves, crushed
- 1 tsp Pomegranate molasses or lemon juice
- 1 pinch Salt
- 1 pinch Pepper

METHOD-FILLING
1 Put the water in a frying pan, add the oil, the rice washed and drained, add the salt. Bring to the boil and cook covered on a low heat for 10 min.
2 Take off the heat, add the meat, the garlic, the pomegranate molasses or lemon juice, the pepper, then mix well and set aside.

METHOD-ASSEMBLY-COOKING
1 Empty the inside of the aubergines with a potato peeler being careful not to pierce the bottom or the sides Fig. 1, 2, 3.
2 Fill the emptied aubergines with the filling, stopping 2 cm from the top so the filling does not spill out when cooking. Set aside. Fig. 4, 5, 6.
3 Heat the oil in a casserole and fry the aubergines on all sides over a low heat.
4 Add the 400 ml of water, garlic, pomegranate molasses or lemon juice, salt, pepper and sugar if used.
To stop the filling spilling out cover the aubergines with a heat proof plate inside the casserole (only use for on the hob method).
5 Cover and leave to simmer for 40 min to allow the aubergines to turn into a confit (caramelise). Check the seasoning and adjust to your taste.
Alternatively after frying, place in an oven proof dish cover with baking parchment then aluminium foil. Cook in a preheated oven at 180° C (gas mark 4) for 40 to 45 min. Uncover and cook for another 10 min. approximately.

ADVICE
We always recommend that the aubergines should not be too big and they should always be well emptied. If you have the possibility of buying small aubergines, they will be easier to empty. This dish is best enjoyed the next day.

SUGGESTIONS
You can replace the minced meat by minced chicken. Serve with a moussaka.

Aubergines with vegetarian filling

PREPARATION 30 MIN COOKING 1 H
INGREDIENTS (SERVES 4)
• 8 Aubergines, small and long (600 g approx.)
black or white or 4 Large aubergines sliced in 2
• 3 tbsp Oil
• 400 ml Water
• 1 Garlic clove, crushed
• 1 tsp Pomegranate molasses or lemon juice
• 1 pinch Salt
• 1 pinch Pepper
• 1 pinch Sugar (optional)

FILLING
• 60 g Rice
• 40 g Soya mince (fine) or replace by 40 g of rice
• 2 Garlic cloves, crushed
• 2 tbsp Oil
• 200 ml Water
• 2 tbsp Lemon juice
• 1 tsp Pomegranate molasses or lemon juice
• 1 pinch Salt
• 1 pinch Pepper

METHOD-FILLING

Put the rice washed and drained in a frying pan with the water, soya mince, garlic, oil, lemon juice, pomegranate molasses or additional lemon juice, salt and pepper.
Cover and cook on a low heat for 10 min. until complete evaporation of the water.

METHOD-ASSEMBLY-COOKING

See preceding recipe for Aubergines Filled With Meat

ADVICE

We always recommend that the aubergines should not be too big and they should always be well emptied. If you have the possibility of buying small aubergines, they will be easier to empty. This dish is best enjoyed the next day.

SUGGESTION

Serve with a moussaka.

Bamia Stew

Okra Stew

PREPARATION 10 MIN COOKING 35 MIN
INGREDIENTS (SERVES 4)

- 400 g Bamia frozen or 500 g fresh
- 3 Garlic cloves cut up small
- 1 tbsp Lemon juice
- 3 tbsp Oil
- 1 tbsp Tomato purée (concentrate)
- 2 Tamarind pods (fresh) peel, stone and retain the paste
or 1 pinch of sugar (both optional)
- 1 pinch Salt
- 1 pinch Pepper
- 400 ml Water or stock of meat or chicken

METHOD

1 Scold the bamia and drain if frozen.

2 Put the oil in a casserole add the bamia, garlic and salt. Cover, sautée and shake at regular intervals on a low heat for 10 min. avoiding stirring so that the okra retains its shape.

3 Add the tomato purée, tamarind, lemon juice, pepper, sugar (if used), water and simmer covered for 25 min.

ADVICE

Cook the day before eating as it is always tastier the next day.

If you are using fresh bamia, wash first then drain without scolding.

Top and tail the bamia (okra) by peeling the cone end and removing the little point at the other end.

To cook proceed the same as for the frozen bamia.

Tamarind adds a sweet and sour taste and possesses numerous health benefits.

To use break the pod, remove the stone and retain the paste.

SUGGESTION

Best served with rice.

The bamia is available fresh in some supermarkets or frozen in ethnic stores.

The fresh tamarind and paste are available in ethnic stores.

Beda be lamouna
Egg and lemon sauce

**PREPARATION 10 MIN COOKING 15 MIN
INGREDIENTS (SERVES 4)**

- 300 ml Chicken stock or Water + 2 tbsp Oil
- 2 tbsp lemon juice
- 1 Egg
- 2 Cardamom pods
- 1 tbsp Cornflour (11 g approx.)
- 100 ml Water (for diluting the cornflour)
- 1 pinch Turmeric
- 1 pinch Salt

METHOD

1 Put the chicken stock or the water and oil in a saucepan,
add the lemon juice, cardamom, turmeric, the salt and bring to the boil.
Allow to boil for 5 min, turn off the heat, remove the cardamom seeds and set aside.
2 Dilute the cornflour with the 100 ml of water in a bowl.
Add the beaten egg, mix well and then add the reserved stock.
3 Put the whole mix over moderate heat, bring to the boil stirring
continuously for 5 min. approximately until the sauce has thickened.
Remove from the heat and pour into 4 ramekins.

ADVICE

Can be served hot or cold on a bed of hot rice. If lumps have formed during
the cooking, put through a chinois strainer or use an electric hand blender
or food processor to obtain a smooth sauce.

ORIGINAL RECIPE

To thicken the sauce, we used to add flour, we have now
replaced it with cornflour for a healthier and lighter sauce.

Chard / Spinach

PREPARATION 10 MIN COOKING 15 MIN
INGREDIENTS (SERVES 4)

- 500 g Chard or spinach (fresh or frozen)
- 1 Onion chopped (70-80 g)
- 2 tbsp Oil
- 3 tbsp Water
- 1 pinch Salt
- 1 pinch Pepper

METHOD

1 Wash and cut the chard or spinach and set aside.

2 Put the oil in a pan and soften the chopped onion til transluscent .
Add the chard or spinach, the water and the salt.

3 Cover and steam in its own juice on a low heat for 10 to15 min.

4 Add the pepper, check and adjust the seasoning to your taste.

SUGGESTION

At the end of the cooking you can add some cooked chick peas, thinly sliced
mushrooms and allow to cook for a further 5 min.

Leek rissoles with meat / chicken / tofu

PREPARATION 60 MIN
COOKING 30 MIN
INGREDIENTS (16 PIECES)
- 300 g Leeks washed and finely sliced
- 150 g Minced meat / minced chicken or tofu mashed
- 30 g Breadcrumbs
- 1 Egg beaten
- 500 ml Water
- 1 pinch Salt
- 1 pinch Pepper

SAUCE
- Leek water saved from cooking
- 1 tbsp Lemon juice
- ½ tsp Turmeric
- 1 pinch Salt
- 1 pinch Pepper
- ½ tsp Sugar (optional)
- 60 ml Oil (for frying)

METHOD

1 Put the leeks in a casserole with the 500ml of water and the pinch of salt.
Cover, bring to the boil and then simmer for 10 min.
2 Drain the leeks in a sieve and retain the cooking liquid. Set aside.

SAUCE

Put the cooking liquid in a casserole, add the lemon juice,
the turmeric, the pepper and set aside.

RISSOLES

1 Mix all the ingredients together in a bowl, the meat or chicken or tofu,
the cooked leeks, the breadcrumbs, the beaten egg, salt and pepper,
making sure the whole lot is thoroughly mixed.
2 Coat your hands lightly with oil and form the mixture into balls of 4 cm
in diameter and flatten gently to make rissoles of 1.5 cm thick
approximately. You should end up with about 16 rissoles.
3 Put the oil in a frying pan and fry the rissoles on both sides.
Put them in the casserole containing the sauce and simmer for 20 min.

ADVICE

May be frozen once cooked.

ORIGINAL RECIPE

Used to be made mainly with meat.

Kebabs of meat / chicken

PREPARATION 20 MIN COOKING 15 MIN
INGREDIENTS (SERVES 4)

- 500 g Meat Steak ou chicken escalope
- 1 Onion (100 g approx.)
- 1 Red pepper
- 1 Green pepper
- 4 Cherry tomatoes
- 1 pinch Salt
- 1 pinch Pepper

METHOD

1 Dice in chunks the peppers and the onion,
cut the meat in cubes and season with salt and pepper.
2 Skewer all the ingredients, alternating the meat, peppers,
tomatoes and onion dividing them equally in between the skewers.
Use 4 or 8 skewers depending on how much you put on each one.
3 Heat a cast iron griddle over a medium heat, place the skewers
on top and grill on all sides turning them frequently.

ADVICE

If you are using wooden skewers, soak them in water
for 10 min before use to stop them burning while grilling.

ORIGINAL RECIPE

The kebabs used to be grilled on a barbecue over charcoal.

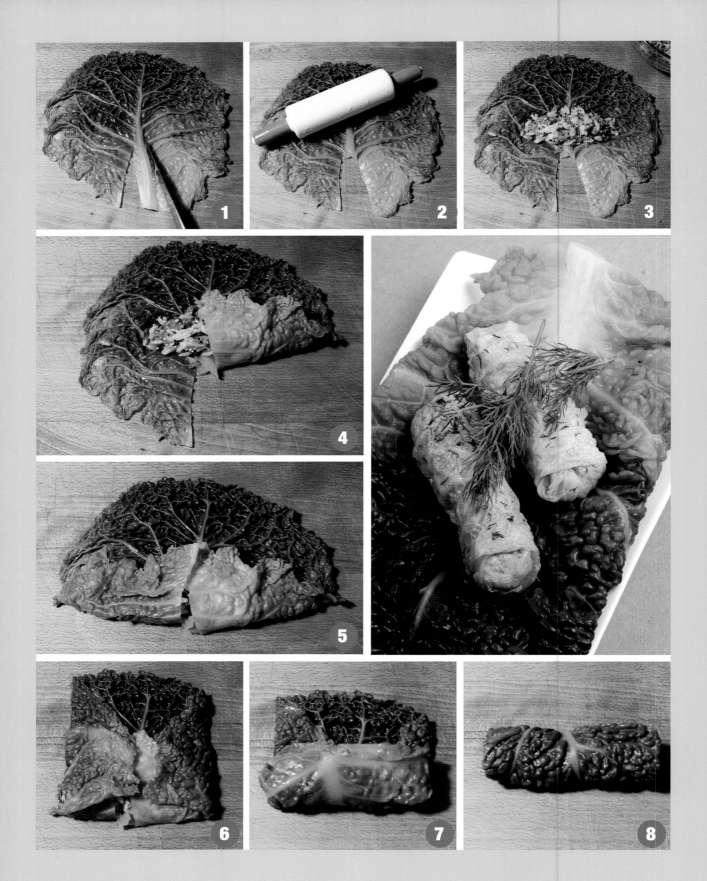

Cabbage leaves with meat filling

PREPARATION 40 MIN
COOKING 55 MIN
INGREDIENTS (12 PIECES)

- 12 Cabbage leaves (small curly cabbage 700 to 800 g)
- 1 tbsp Lemon juice
- 2 tbsp Oil
- 250 ml Water
- 1 tbsp Dill, chopped (optional)
- 1 pinch Turmeric
- 1 pinch Salt

FILLING

- 100 g Minced meat
- 30 g Rice
- 1 Onion, chopped (50 to 60 g)
- 1 Garlic clove, crushed
- 2 tbsp Lemon juice
- 1 tbsp Oil
- 100 ml Water
- 1 pinch Salt
- 1 pinch Pepper

METHOD-FILLING

Put the water in a frying pan, add the oil, the rice washed and drained then the salt.

Cover and allow to cook for 10 min until the complete evaporation of the water.

Take off the heat, add all the other ingredients of the filling, mix and set aside.

METHOD-ASSEMBLY-COOKING

1 Detach the 12 cabbage leaves, wash them and soak them
in salted boiling water for 2 to 3 min, allowing them to soften.

2 Drain and refresh them in cold water.

3 Lay a cabbage leaf over the worktop smooth side up,
cut off the thick end of the stem with a knife then flatten it with a rolling pin Fig. 1, 2.
Place 1 tablespoon of filling in the centre of the leaf Fig. 3, fold the leaf over Fig. 4, 5, fold over
2 cm each side into the centre Fig. 6 then roll tightly to form a roll of 7 to
8 cm approximately Fig. 7, 8. Pack the rolls tightly side by side in a casserole finished ends
down to stop them unravelling.
Drizzle the oil over the cabbage rolls, add salt and dill if used,
turmeric and the 250 ml of water.

4 Cover the rolls with an oven proof plate inside the pan to stop
the cabbage rolls opening up while cooking.

5 Cover the casserole, bring to the boil, then simmer for 40 min.
Taste the sauce and adjust the seasoning if required.

SUGGESTION

You can replace the meat with minced chicken.

Cabbage leaves with vegetarian filling

PREPARATION 40 MIN COOKING 55 MIN
INGREDIENTS (12 PIECES)

- 12 Cabbage leaves (small curly cabbage 700 to 800 g)
- 1 tbsp Lemon juice
- 2 tbsp Oil
- 250 ml Water
- 1 tbsp Dill (optional)
- 1 pinch Turmeric
- 1 pinch Salt

FILLING
- 50 g Rice
- 25 g Soya mince (fine) or replaced by 25 g of rice
- 1 Onion, chopped (50 to 60 g)
- 2 Garlic cloves crushed
- 1 tbsp Lemon juice
- 3 tbsp Oil
- 250 ml Water
- 1 pinch Salt
- 1 pinch Pepper

METHOD-FILLING

Put the 3 tablespoons of oil in a frying pan and sweat the onion over moderate heat until soft and translucent. Add the rest of the filling ingredients and mix well. Allow to cook until complete evaporation of the water.

METHOD-ASSEMBLY-COOKING

See preceding recipe for "Cabbage with meat filling".

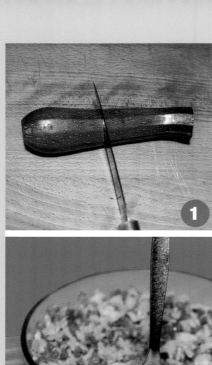

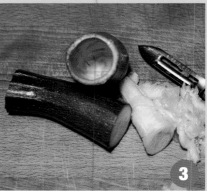

Courgettes with meat filling

Traditional recipe

PREPARATION 40 MIN
COOKING 50 MIN
INGREDIENTS (SERVES 4)
- 8 Small courgettes or 4 medium courgettes (500 to 700 g) cut in 2
- 1 tbsp Oil
- 2 tbsp Lemon juice
- 300 ml Water
- 1 pinch Salt
- 1 tsp Dried mint (powder)

FILLING
- 150 g Minced meat
- 40 g Rice
- 2 Garlic cloves crushed
- 2 tsp Dried mint (powder)
- 1 tbsp Oil
- 150 ml Water
- 3 tbsp Lemon juice
- 1 pinch Salt
- 1 pinch Pepper

METHOD-FILLING

Put the water in a frying pan, add the oil, the rice washed and drained and the salt. Cover and cook on a low heat for 10 min. until complete evaporation of the water. Take off the heat and add all the other filling ingredients. Mix well and set aside.

METHOD-ASSEMBLY-COOKING

1 Wash the courgettes, trim both ends. With a potato peeler hollow out the courgettes by removing the pulp taking care not to pierce the end and the skin Fig. 1, 2, 3. Save the pulpe of the courgettes for another recipe.

2 Fill the courgettes using a teaspoon Fig. 4, compacting the fillng well down up to 1 to 2 cm from the edge Fig. 5, 6 to stop the rice spilling out whilst cooking. Tightly pack the bottom of a casserole with the filled courgettes.

3 Add the lemon juice, mint, oil, salt and water. To stop the filling spilling out during the cooking, cover the top of the courgettes with an oven proof plate.

4 Cover the casserole and simmer for 40 min. approximately. Keep watching the cooking, if necessary add more water. Taste the sauce and adjust the seasoning if required. Alternatively place in an oven proof dish (omitting the oven proof plate) cover with baking parchment then aluminium foil. Cook in a preheated oven at 180° C (gas mark 4) for 40 to 45 min. Uncover and cook for another 10 min. approximately.

ADVICE

We always recommend that the courgettes should not be too large, and should be well hollowed out. If you have the choice, buy small courgettes, they are easier to hollow out. This dish is tastier the next day.
Keep the pulp for "Pulp of courgettes" recipe.

SUGGESTIONS

Serve with the cooked courgettes pulp (see recipe page 137).
You can substitute minced chicken with minced meat.

Courgettes with vegetarian filling

PREPARATION 50 MIN COOKING 50 MIN
INGREDIENTS (SERVES 4)
- 8 Small courgette or 4 medium courgettes (500 to 700 g) cut in 2
- 1 tbsp Oil
- 2 tbsp Lemon juice
- 300 ml Water
- 1 pinch Salt
- 1 tsp Dried mint (powder)

FILLING
- 1 Onion, chopped (80 g approx.)
- 15 g Soya mince (fine) or replace by 15 g of rice
- 25 g Rice
- 3 Garlic cloves, crushed
- 2 tsp Dried mint (powder)
- 150 ml Water
- 3 tbsp Oil
- 2 tbsp Lemon juice
- 1 pinch Salt
- 1 pinch Pepper

METHOD-FILLING

1 In a casserole, put the oil and over a medium heat
add the onion and soften till soft and translucent.
2 Add the water, mint, garlic, soya mince, lemon juice, salt, pepper,
the rice washed and drained. Bring to the boil, cover and allow to cook on a low heat
for 10 min., take off the heat and set aside.

ASSEMBLY-COOKING
See preceding recipe for "Courgettes with meat filling ".

ADVICE
We always recommend that the courgettes should not be too large, and should be well
hollowed out. If you have the choice, buy small courgettes, they are easier to hollow
out. This dish is tastier the next day.
Keep the pulp for "Pulp of courgettes" recipe.

SUGGESTION
Serve with the "Pulp of courgette" (see recipe page 137).

Courgette cheese gratin

PREPARATION 15 MIN COOKING 50 MIN
INGREDIENTS (SERVES 4-5)

- 3 Courgettes (600 g approx.)
- 1 Onion, chopped (60 g approx.)
- 3 tbsp Oil
- 2 tbsp Water
- 120 g Cheese, grated, (cheddar, gruyere, parmesan or other) or tofu mashed
with a fork (reserve 10 g of cheese for sprinkling over the top)
- 2 Eggs
- 1 tbsp Breadcrumbs
- 1 pinch Salt
- 1 pinch Pepper

METHOD

1 Put the oil in a medium casserole over gentle heat, add the onion and cook until soft and translucent. Add the washed and diced courgettes with the water and salt. Cover and sauté the courgettes, allowing them to cook in their own juice for 20 min. approximately, ensuring that they don't stick to the pan.

2 Mix the beaten eggs with the cheese or the tofu in a bowl, add the pepper and set aside.

3 Put the cooked courgettes in an oven proof dish (21 cm x 21 cm approx.),
add the egg cheese mixture and mix carefully, sprinkle with the reserved grated cheese and the breadcrumbs. Place in a preheated oven at 180° C (gas mark 4) for 30 min. approximately, until golden brown.

ORIGINAL RECIPE

The courgette cheese gratin used to contain more eggs and cheese.

Courgette : pulp of courgettes

Retrieved from recipes
for filled courgettes

PREPARATION 10 MIN COOKING 15 MIN
INGREDIENTS (SERVES 4)
- The pulp of courgettes (retrieved from the inside of the filled courgettes)
- 1 Onion, chopped (50 g approx.)
- 3 tbsp Oil
- 2 tbsp Water
- ½ tsp Turmeric
- 1 pinch Salt
- 1 pinch Pepper

METHOD

1 Put the oil in a small casserole, add the onion
and cook over moderate heat until soft and translucent.

2 Add the courgette pulp with the water, turmeric, salt and pepper.
Cover and simmer for 10 to 15 min.

SUGGESTION

Is usually served as a vegetable, as an accompaniment to main courses or is served on
its own as a light snack just with yoghurt or some labna (see recipe page 52).

Courgettes sautéed

PREPARATION 10 MIN COOKING 15 MIN
INGREDIENTS (SERVES 4)

- 500 g Courgettes
- 1 Onion, chopped (70 g approx.)
- 2 tbsp Oil
- 2 tbsp Water
- 1 pinch Salt
- 1 pinch Pepper

METHOD

1 Wash and dice the courgettes in large chunks.

2 Put the oil in a casserole, add the chopped onion and cook over a medium heat until soft and translucent. Add the courgettes, salt, pepper and water.

Cover and simmer on a low heat for 15 min. approximately.

Sauté (lightly shake) the courgettes at regular interval, ensuring they don't stick to the bottom of the pan.

Take off the heat, taste and adjust the seasoning if required.

SUGGESTION

Quick recipe to be served as a light meal with grated cheese, yoghurt or as an accompaniment to main courses.

Escalopes of grilled chicken

PREPARATION 5 MIN COOKING 10 MIN
INGREDIENTS (SERVES 4)

- 4 Escalopes of chicken breast
- 1 Onion (100 g approx.)
- 1 pinch Paprika (mild)
- 1 pinch Salt
- 1 pinch Pepper

METHOD

Put the thick sliced onion with the salt in a large heated frying pan or griddle.
Grill over medium heat for a few minutes. Add the escalopes, the pepper and the
paprika. Allow to grill for 10 min. approximately, turning the
escalopes from time to time until cooked and golden on both sides.

SUGGESTION

Quick recipe to be served as a main course with the addition of vegetables.

Vine leaves with meat filling
Traditional recipe

PREPARATION 60 MIN
COOKING 45 MIN
INGREDIENTS (30 PIECES APPROX.)
- 180 g Vine leaves vacuum packed or in sealed jars.
- 1 tbsp Oil
- 400 ml Water
- ½ tsp Sugar (optional)
- 1 tsp Dried mint (powder)

MEAT FILLING
- 180 g Minced meat
- 70 g Rice
- 2 Garlic cloves crushed
- 1 tbsp Oil
- 100 ml Water
- 1 tsp Lemon juice
- 1 tsp Dried mint (powdert)
- 1 pinch Salt
- 1 pinch Pepper

METHOD-FILLING

Put the water in a frying pan add the oil, the rice washed and drained and the salt. Cook covered for 10 min. on a low heat. Take off the heat, add the rest of the filling ingredients. Mix thoroughly and set aside.

METHOD-ASSEMBLY-COOKING

1 Wash the vine leaves thoroughly to remove the preserving salt and brine then drain in a colander.
2 Place a vine leaf flat on a work surface smooth side down. With a rolling pin flatten and crush the veins and cut the stalk off at the base of the leaf Fig. 1, 2.
3 Place 2 teaspoons (approx.) of filling over the wide part of the leaf Fig. 3. Fold the base and the sides of the leaf over to cover the filling Fig. 4, 5, 6. Roll the remainder of the leaf into a cigar shape of 7 cm long (approx.) Fig. 7, 8.
4 Tightly pack the stuffed vine leaves in a casserole, finished ends down to stop them unravelling. Add the seasoning, the oil, sugar, mint and water.

5 Place an oven proof plate inside the pan to cover the vine leaves in order to keep them whole and to stop them opening.
6 Cover the casserole and allow to cook over a gentle heat for 35 min. approx.
During the cooking process, check the water level and the seasoning.
Taste the sauce and adjust if required.
Alternatively place in a covered oven proof dish (omitting the oven proof plate) cover with baking parchment then
aluminium foil. Cook in a preheated oven at 180° C (gas mark 4) for 40 to 45 min. Uncover and cook for another 10 min. approximately.

ADVICE

Cook the day before consuming to enable the flavours to fully develop. Can also be frozen once cooked.

SUGGESTION

The vine leaves can be served as an hors d'oeuvre or mezze, or as an accompaniment to a main course. You can substitute the minced meat with minced chicken.

Vine leaves with vegetarian filling

PREPARATION 60 MIN COOKING 45 MIN
INGREDIENTS (30 PIECES APPROX.)

- 150 g Vine leaves vacuum packed or in sealed jars
- 2 tbsp Oil
- 400 ml Water
- ½ tsp Sugar (optional)
- 1 tsp Dried mint (powder)

VEGETARIAN FILLING

- 110 g Rice
- 1 Onion, finely chopped (100 g approx.)
- 50 g Tofu or replace by 25 g rice
- 2 Garlic cloves crushed
- 3 tbsp Oil
- 1 tsp Lemon juice
- 150 ml Water
- 1 tsp Dried mint (powder)
- 1 pinch Salt
- 1 pinch Pepper

METHOD - FILLING

1 Put the oil in a casserole and sweat the onion till soft and translucent.

2 Add the water, the rice washed and drained (add 25 g more rice if tofu is not used), the lemon juice, garlic, salt, pepper and the mint. Cover and cook on a gentle heat for 10 min.

3 Take off the heat, if used add the tofu mashed with a fork and set aside.

ASSEMBLY - COOKING

See preceding recipe "Vine leaves with meat filling".

ADVICE

Cook the day before consuming to enable the flavours to fully develop.
Can also be frozen once cooked.

SUGGESTIONS

The vine leaves can be served as an hors d'oeuvre or mezze, or as an accompaniment to a main course.
Can also be served with yoghurt or "Labna" (see recipe page 52)

Broad bean casserole

PREPARATION 20 MIN COOKING 45 MIN

INGREDIENTS (SERVES 4)

- 1 kg Broad beans
- 3 Garlic cloves
- 3 tbsp Oil
- 400 ml Water or stock of meat or chicken
- 1 pinch Salt
- 1 pinch Pepper
- ½ tsp Sugar (optional)
- Fresh coriander, a few chopped sprigs (optional)

METHOD

1 Pod the beans to the exception of the ones with young bright and tender skins that you will cut into small chunks.
Wash and leave to drain in a colander.

2 Put the oil in a casserole, add the beans, the salt and the garlic peeled and cut into small pieces. Cover, sauté and shake at regular interval on a low heat for 10 min.

3 Add the water or stock of meat or chicken, pepper, sugar and the coriander if used. Cover and allow to simmer on a low heat for 35 min. approx. Check the cooking and add more water if necessary.

4 Taste and adjust the seasoning if required.

SUGGESTION

Serve sprinkled with fresh chopped coriander, with rice, meat or chicken.

ORIGINAL RECIPE

It used to be small tender and sweet beans that we used to cook whole with the skin. They never required the addition of sugar.

Green beans
with tomato casserole

PREPARATION 10 MIN COOKING 45 MIN
INGREDIENTS (SERVES 4)

- 700 g Green beans fresh or frozen (if frozen, blanch and drain)
- 1 Onion, chopped (70-80 g)
- 3 tbsp Oil
- 1 tbsp Tomato purée (concentrate)
- 450 ml Water or stock of meat or chicken
- 1 pinch Salt
- 1 pinch Pepper

METHOD

1 Put the oil in a casserole and sweat the onion until soft and translucent.

2 Add the washed and drained beans with the salt. Cover, sauté and shake the beans regularly over a medium heat for 15 min approximately.

Add the tomato purée, the water and pepper. Cover and simmer for 30 min.

SUGGESTION

Ideal served with rice.

Koftas of bakala fish
Cod fish rissoles

PREPARATION 25 MIN
FRYING 10 MIN COOKING 35 MIN
INGREDIENTS (12 PIECES)

- 200 g Cod, dried and desalted (bakala)
  or raw fish filet fresh or frozen
- 50 g Breadcrumbs
- 2 Eggs
- 1 Garlic clove crushed
- 200 ml Water
- ½ tsp Cumin powder
- 1 pinch Salt
- 1 pinch Pepper

SAUCE

- 200 ml Water
- 1 tbsp Tomato purée (concentrate)
- 3 tbsp Lemon juice
- 2 Garlic cloves crushed
- ½ tsp Cumin powder
- 1 pinch Salt
- 1 pinch Pepper
- 4 tbsp Oil (for frying)

METHOD

1 Place the fish in a casserole with the 200 ml of water,
bring to the boil and cook over a moderate heat for 10 min.
2 Drain the fish and reserve the stock.
3 In a bowl, mash the drained fish with a fork and mix with the crushed garlic, the cumin, the beaten
eggs, the breadcrumbs, salt and pepper. Mix all the ingredients thoroughly.
4 Shape 12 rissoles, of 4 cm in diameter and 1 cm thick, then set aside.

SAUCE

Put the 200 ml of water in a casserole with the reserved fish stock, the cumin, tomato purée,
crushed garlic, lemon juice, salt and pepper. Bring to the boil for 5 min. and set aside.

COOKING

1 Heat the oil in a medium frying pan and lightly fry the rissoles on both sides.
2 Place them in the casserole with the sauce, cover and simmer gently on a low heat for 20 min.
Check the seasoning and if required adjust to your taste.

SUGGESTION

Best served with rice and vegetables.

ORIGINAL RECIPE

Used to be made only with dried desalted cod (bakala).

Koftas of meat or chicken
Rissoles

PREPARATION 30 MIN COOKING 15 MIN
INGREDIENTS (12 PIECES)

- 400 g Minced meat or minced chicken breast
- 20 g Bulgar wheat, fine (optional)
- 1 Onion, chopped (100 g approx.)
- 1 bunch Parsley (flat), chopped
- 3 tbsp Oil
- 1 pinch Salt
- 1 pinch Pepper

METHOD

1 If using bulgar wheat, wash it in a sieve.

2 Place the washed bulgar wheat in a bowl with 1 tablespoon of water and allow to rest for 15 min.

3 Mix all the ingredients in a bowl, the minced meat or minced chicken, the chopped onion, the chopped parsley, the oil, the bulgar wheat (if used), the salt and pepper.
Coat your hands with oil, form the mix into 12 balls, each the size of a walnut then flatten to form rissoles.

4 Heat a cast iron griddle pan over a medium heat, lay the rissoles on it and grill on both sides for 15 min. approximately.

SUGGESTIONS

You can also fry them in a frying pan with a little oil.
You can make them into grilled skewered kebabs.

Lahma bel ma'ala with meat
Traditional recipe
(Middle eastern ratatouille)

PREPARATION 20 MIN COOKING 50 MIN
INGREDIENTS (SERVES 4)
- 350 g Meat ragout (see recipe page 176)
- 2 Potatoes (180 to 200 g)
- 1 Onion (150 g approx.)
- 1 Aubergine (300 g approx.)
- 12 Dried prunes or dried apricots soaked in boiling water
- 1 Tomato (100 g approx.)
- 2 tbsp Lemon juice
- 4 tbsp Oil
- 1 tsp Tomato purée (concentrate)
- 2 Tamarind pods (fresh), peel, stone and retain the paste (optional)
- 450 ml Water
- 1 pinch Salt
- 1 pinch Pepper

METHOD

1 Put the oil in a casserole, add all the vegetables peeled and diced in chunks, the onion, the potatoes, the tomato and the aubergine. Add the salt, cover, sauté and shake over a gentle heat for 10 min.

2 Add the meat ragout, the prunes or apricots, the tomato purée, the tamarind (if used), the lemon juice, the pepper and the water.
Cover and simmer for 30 to 40 min. Taste and adjust the seasoning if required.

ADVICE

You can also substitute the meat for chicken.
Tamarind adds a sweet and sour taste and possesses numerous health benefits. To use, break the pod, remove the stone and retain the paste.

Lahma bel ma'ala vegetarian
(Middle eastern ratatouille)

PREPARATION 20 MIN COOKING 50 MIN
INGREDIENTS (SERVES 4)
- 2 Potatoes (180 to 200 g)
- 1 Onion (150 g approx.)
- 1 Aubergine (300 g approx.)
- 60 g Tofu cut up in small cubes (optional)
- 12 Dried prunes or dried apricots soaked in boiling water
- 1 Tomato (100 g approx.)
- 2 tbsp Lemon juice
- 4 tbsp Oil
- 1 tsp tomato purée (concentrate)
- 1 or 2 Tamarind pods (fresh), peel, stone and retain the paste (optional)
- 450 ml Water
- 1 pinch Salt
- 1 pinch Pepper

METHOD

1 Put the oil in a casserole, add all the vegetables peeled and diced in chunks,
the onion, the potatoes, the tomato and the aubergine with the tofu if used.
Add the salt, cover, sauté and shake over gentle heat for 10 min.
2 Add the prunes or apricots, the tomato purée, the tamarind if used,
the lemon juice, the pepper and water. Cover and simmer for 30 to 40 min.
Taste and adjust the seasoning if required.

ORIGINAL RECIPE
Always used to be made with meat whence its name (lahma in arabic means meat).

ADVICE
Just as with the pomegranate, tamarind possesses numerous health
benefits. Tamarind adds a sweet and sour taste.
To use break the pod, remove the stone and retain the paste.

Moussaka with meat
Traditional recipe

PREPARATION 20 MIN COOKING 45 MIN
INGREDIENTS (SERVES 4)
- 3 Aubergines (700 to 800 g)
- 200 ml Water
- 100 ml Oil (for frying)

FILLING
- 150 g Minced meat
- 2 tsp Tomato purée (concentrate)
- 2 tbsp Oil
- 3 Garlic cloves finely cut
- 50 ml Water
- 1 pinch Salt
- 1 pinch Pepper
- 15 g Pine nuts (optional)

METHOD-AUBERGINES

Peel, wash and slice the aubergines in 1 cm thick approximately. Place the slices on the oven tray. With a pastry brush, coat them with oil on both sides, grill for 5 to 10 min. approximately on each side. When they are nice and golden, remove from the grill and set aside.

METHOD-FILLING

Put the oil in a frying pan, add the minced meat and stir fry over medium heat for 5 min., add the 50 ml of water, the tomato purée, the garlic, the salt and pepper. Cover and allow to cook for 10 min. on a low heat. Uncover, stir until complete evaporation of the water and set aside.

METHOD-ASSEMBLY

Cover the bottom of a casserole with the grilled aubergines, layer with some of the filling, then with the rest of the aubergines and finish with the remainder of the filling. Add the 200 ml of water, the salt and the pepper. Allow to cook on a low heat for 25 min. approximately.
If you are using the oven method, assemble the moussaka in an oven proof dish, cover with baking parchment then aluminium foil. Place in the preheated oven at180 ° C (gas mark 4) for 20 to 25 min. Uncover and allow to cook for a further 10 min. approximately.
Just before the end of the cooking add the pine nuts if used (about 2 min. before the end).

ORIGINAL RECIPE

The aubergines used to be deep fried, they absorbed too much oil and became heavy to digest.

Moussaka vegetarian
Aubergines with soya mince

PREPARATION 20 MIN COOKING 55 MIN
INGREDIENTS (SERVES 4)
- 3 Aubergines (700 to 800 g)
- 200 ml Water
- 100 ml Oil (for frying)

FILLING
- 1 Onion finely chopped (40 g approx.)
- 20 g Tofu mashed with a fork
- 30 g Soya mince (fine)
- 2 tsp Tomato purée (concentrate)
- 3 Garlic cloves finely sliced
- 50 ml Oil
- 100 ml Water
- 1 pinch Salt
- 1 pinch Pepper
- 15 g Pine nuts (optional)

METHOD-AUBERGINES

Peel, wash and silce the aubergines in1 cm thick. Place the slices on the oven tray.
With a pastry brush, coat both sides with oil, grill for 5 to 10 min. approximately on each
side. When they are nicely golden remove from the grill and set aside.

METHOD-FILLING

Put the oil in a frying pan, add the onion and sweat until soft and translucent, add the
water, tofu, soya mince, tomato purée, garlic, salt and pepper. Cover and allow to cook on a
gentle heat for 10 min. Uncover and stir until complete evaporation of the water.

METHOD-ASSEMBLY

See preceding recipe " Moussaka with meat " (page 159).

ORIGINAL RECIPE

The aubergines used to be deep fried,
they absorbed too much oil and became heavy to digest.

Fish in lemon sauce

PREPARATION 15 MIN COOKING 30 MIN
INGREDIENTS (SERVES 4)
- 4 Fish steaks (cod, halibut, hake, salmon, or other)
- 1 Celery stalk (rib) cut into chunks
- 2 Garlic cloves thinly sliced
- 2 tbsp Lemon juice
- ½ tsp Cumin powder
- ½ tsp Turmeric
- 150 ml Water
- 1 pinch Salt

METHOD

1 Put the water in a casserole, add all the ingredients except for the fish, bring to the boil and simmer covered for 15 min. approximately.

2 Lower the heat completely, add the fish steaks, simmer covered for 8 min. approximately. Turn the steaks over and simmer for a further 5 min. approximately. Taste and adjust the seasoning if required, serve immediately.

ADVICE

Check that the fish does not overcook
so that the flesh remains soft and moist.

SUGGESTION

Serve with rice or potatoes.

Oven baked fish

With potatoes and tomatoes

PREPARATION 15 MIN COOKING 50 MIN
INGREDIENTS (SERVES 4)
- 1 kg (approx.) Fish, whole sea bass or sea bream or any other whole fish scaled, gutted and washed
- 4 Potatoes, sliced (300 g approx.)
- 1 Tomato, sliced (100 g approx.)
- 3 tbsp Lemon juice
- 1 Onion, sliced (70 g approx.)
- 3 Garlic cloves diced
- ½ tsp Cumin powder
- ½ tsp Turmeric
- 2 tbsp Oil
- 250 ml Water
- 1 pinch Salt

METHOD

1 Place the fish in an oven proof dish, add the potatoes peeled and sliced 1 cm thick, the tomato, onion, garlic, lemon juice, cumin, turmeric, oil, water and salt.

2 Cover with baking parchment first, then with foil so as not to let the fish come into contact with the aluminium foil. Place the fish in the preheated oven at 175°C (gas mark 3 ½) and bake for 30 to 40 min. Uncover the dish and cook for a further 10 min. to allow the fish to roast and brown.

Peppers filled
with meat / chicken or tofu

PREPARATION 30 MIN COOKING 50 MIN
INGREDIENTS (SERVES 4)
- 4 Peppers green, red or other (450 g approx.) or 8 small peppers
- 2 tbsp Oil
- 250 ml Water
- 2 tsp Dried mint (powder)
- 1 tbsp Lemon juice
- 1 pinch Salt
- 1 pinch Pepper

FILLING
- 100g Minced meat, minced chicken or tofu
- 60g Rice
- 3 tbsp Oil
- 1 Onion, chopped (80g approx.)
- 2 Garlic cloves, crushed
- 150 ml Water
- 1 tsp Dried mint (powder)
- 1 tbsp Lemon juice
- 1 pinch Salt

METHOD-FILLING
1 Put the oil in a frying pan, over a moderate heat add the onion and sweat until soft and translucent.
2 Add the 150 ml of water, the mint, the garlic, lemon juice, salt, pepper and the washed and drained rice. Cover, bring to the boil and cook on a low heat for 10 min. until complete evaporation of the water.
3 Add the minced meat or minced chicken or tofu, mix well and set aside.

METHOD-ASSEMBLY-COOKING
1 Wash then cut about 1 cm off the top of the peppers on the green stalk side (keep the cut off end with the stalk to place back as a lid on the stuffed pepper prior to cooking if you wish). Empty the inside of the peppers, the seeds as well as the white pith.
2 With a teaspoon fill the peppers, packing them lightly up to 2 cm from the top so the filling does not spill over whilst cooking.
3 Lay the peppers side by side in a casserole, add the oil, water, mint, lemon juice, salt and pepper.
4 To stop the filling spilling out during cooking, cover with an oven proof plate inside the casserole.
5 Cover the casserole and allow to cook for 30 min. on a low heat.
Taste the sauce and adjust the seasoning if required.
If you are using the oven method, place the peppers in an oven proof dish (omitting the oven proof plate), at this stage you can place the cut off ends with the stalks over the peppers as decoration, cover with baking parchment then aluminium foil, place in the preheated oven at180 ° C (gas mark 4) and cook for 30 to 35 min. Uncover and allow to cook for a further 10 min. approx.

Chicken in lemon sauce

PREPARATION 15 MIN COOKING 50 MIN
INGREDIENTS (SERVES 4)
- 1 Whole or portioned chicken
- 3 tbsp Oil
- 2 tbsp Lemon juice
- 4 Cardamom pods
- ½ tsp Turmeric
- 200 ml Water
- 1 pinch Salt
- 1 pinch Pepper

METHOD

1 Put the oil in a large casserole, add the chicken,
turn and braise on all sides over a medium heat until lightly golden.

2 Add the water, cardamom, turmeric, salt and pepper.

3 Cover and simmer on a low heat for 25 to 35 min., add the lemon juice and allow
to cook for a further 5 min. Taste and adjust the seasoning if required.

ADVICE

The addition of the lemon juice at the beginning would delay the cooking of the chicken.
Where possible we advise free range or organic chickens.

SUGGESTIONS

To avoid braising (frying) the chicken, put all the ingredients (except the lemon juice) in a
large casserole, bring to the boil, add the chicken and simmer for 30 to 35 min. Towards the
end of the cooking, add the lemon juice. This method is quicker and healthier than braising.

Chicken with quinces

PREPARATION 15 MIN COOKING 50 MIN

INGREDIENTS (SERVES 4)
- 1 Whole or portioned chicken
- 2 Quinces
- 3 tbsp Oil
- 2 tbsp Lemon juice
- 4 Cardamom pods
- ½ tsp Turmeric
- 200 ml Water
- 1 pinch Salt
- 1 pinch Pepper
- 1 pinch Sugar (optional)

METHOD

1 Peel, wash and quarter the quinces and set aside.

2 Put the oil in a large casserole, add the chicken,
turn and braise on all sides over a medium heat until lightly golden.

3 Add the water, cardamom, turmeric, salt and pepper.

4 Cover and simmer for 20 min. approx.

5 Add the quinces, the lemon juice, the sugar if used and cook for a
further 20 min. Taste and adjust the seasoning if required.

ADVICE

Where possible we advise free range or organic chickens. The addition of the
lemon juice at the beginning would delay the cooking of the chicken.

SUGGESTION

You can substitute the chicken with meat (beef, lamb, veal).

Chicken with prunes / apricots

PREPARATION 15 MIN COOKING 50 MIN
INGREDIENTS (SERVES 4)
- 1 Whole or portioned chicken
- 200 g Prunes or apricots, stoned
- 3 tbsp Oil
- 2 tbsp Lemon juice
- 4 Cardamom pods
- ½ tsp Turmeric
- 200 ml Water
- 1 pinch Salt
- 1 pinch Pepper

METHOD
1 Wash and soak the prunes or apricots in boiling water for 10 min.

2 Drain them in a colander, rinse under cold water and set aside.

3 Put the oil in a large casserole, add the chicken, turn and braise on all sides over medium heat until lightly golden.

4 Add the water, cardamom, turmeric, salt and pepper.

5 Cover and simmer for 20 min. approx.

6 Add the prunes or apricots, the lemon juice and cook for a further 20 min.
Taste and adjust the seasoning if required.

ADVICE
Where possible we advise free range or organic chickens. The addition of the lemon juice at the beginning would delay the cooking of the chicken.

SUGGESTION
You can substitute the chicken with meat (beef, lamb, veal).

Chicken, roasted

PREPARATION 15 MIN COOKING 70 MIN
INGREDIENTS (SERVES 4)

- 1 Whole chicken
- 300 g Potatoes
- 1 tsp Paprika
- 2 tsp Lemon juice
- 1 tbsp Oil
- 150 ml Water
- 1 pinch Salt
- 1 pinch Pepper

METHOD

1 Using an oven proof dish, mix the seasoning of paprika, lemon juice, salt, pepper and the 1 tablespoon of oil. Add the whole washed chicken and coat it all over with the mix of seasoning.

2 Add the potatoes, peeled, washed and diced in large chunks, together with the 150 ml of water. Cover with grease proof paper then aluminium foil to avoid putting the foil into direct contact with the chicken.

3 Place the dish in the preheated oven at 180 ° C (gas mark 4) for 35 min to 45 min approx.
Remove from the oven, turn the chicken over, cover and replace in the oven for another 15 min.

4 Uncover the chicken and allow it to turn golden brown for another 10 min. on each side.

ADVICE

Covering the chicken during the cooking process, allows it to remain moist. Where possible we advise free range or organic chickens.

Meat ragout
Meat stew casserole

PREPARATION 10 MIN COOKING 60 MIN
INGREDIENTS (SERVES 4)

- 800 g Meat for roasting (joint of beef or other) whole or diced
- 3 tbsp Oil
- 1 Onion, small (60 g approx.)
- 200 ml Water
- 1 pinch Salt
- 1 pinch Pepper

METHOD

1 Put the oil in a casserole on a medium heat,
add the meat whole or cut up in large cubes with the peeled onion
(whole). Turn and braise on all sides.

2 Add the water, the pepper and simmer on a low heat for 50 min.
approximately. Check and increase the timing if required.

3 Add the salt, check and adjust the seasoning to your taste.

ADVICE

Prior to serving the ragout remove the onion.
The onion is only added to the cooking for flavouring.
The addition of salt at the beginning would delay the cooking time.

SUGGESTION

You can retrieve a little of the sauce as a stock
for cooking the accompanying vegetables

NO HOLIDAYS WITHOUT CEREALS AND PULSES

*My mother recalls leaving by limousine amid chaotic scenes
for the "onslaught" of Aboukir a bay near Alexandria 3 hours
from Cairo, where each summer the family
would spend two months vacation.
Picture the scene, as a dozen people, parents, aunts,
children and staff, squashed like sardines into the vehicle did not dare
to complain, as they were only travelling for 3 hours !
They should put up with the inconvenience,
as after all they were going on holiday !
In addition to all their luggage, they had all their pots and pans,
as well as all the sacks of jute filled with lentils, beans, rice, bulgar
wheat, flour, sugar etc.. all they required for the 2 months away.
This entire load was so heavy, that at certain points along the route,
everyone had to get out of the car to enable
the driver to continue the journey.
Faced with this heavy load, the chauffeur highly agitated
and worried they would not be able to reach their destination,
in an air of desperation would appeal to my Grandfather,
"Mr. Sultan, there is everything you need there !
after all you are not going to the desert !"
Imagine, my Grandfather being so fastidious
about the quality of his food, and afraid he would not find all these
provisions locally, prefered to take them all with the entire luggage !*

The pulses

The pulses
Proteins of the poor

Pulses often used to be referred to as "proteins of the poor".
They have long been the staple diet and the main source of protein for the majority
of the population of the "third world", due to their plentiful supply
and low cost compared to meat or chicken.
They have now gained popularity due to their many health benefits, notably their fibre
content and their slow releasing sugars. With the increased demand for vegetarian dishes
and the avoidance of too much meat, they have now been re-established as a protein of
worth and elevated to a higher status. Pulses are an excellent source of protein. When
compared to meat, the proteins are
 "incomplete".
They become "complete" when consumed with cereals.
In the Middle East, they are often eaten with rice or wheat. Pulses are an
important source of nutritional fibre. In order to absorb the iron in the pulses, serve them
with salad, lemon, parsley or other herbs (vitamin C).

They are easy to cook and are always preferable to the tinned pulses which often contain
preservatives. Of course not forgetting and quite important nowadays, they are more eco-
nomical.They are a substitute to animal proteins for
vegetarians.

ADVICE
Beans, dried peas and chick peas should be soaked overnight (about 10 hours), as this
will render them more digestible and reduce flatulence.
Do not add bicarbonate of soda during the soaking or cooking process, as is often advised.
The addition of bicarbonate could hinder the digestion and
assimilition of the minerals and can also alter the flavours.

FUL MEDAMMES
Fava Beans (Little Brown Beans)

*Egyptian national dish, staple diet of the man in the street
but equally appreciated by the whole population.
It is a false notion, that beans are indigestible,
on the contrary we used to consume them puréed or sprouted
as soups when convalescing, as they are full of iron
and easy to digest in this manner.*

*We consume the beans seasoned with salt, olive oil,
lemon juice, accompanied by a middle eastern salad, tahini sauce
(sesame seeds paste) and hard boiled egg. All these ingredients
contribute to the assimilation of minerals in the beans and make it
a complete meal.*

Ful medammes
Fava Beans (Little dried brown beans)

PREPARATION 15 MIN COOKING 60 MIN
INGREDIENTS (SERVES 4)
- 250 g Ful medammes (little dried brown beans)
- 1 Onion, chopped (50 to 60 g)
- 2 Garlic cloves crushed
- 2 tbsp Olive oil
- ½ tsp Paprika mild or hot
- 1 litre Water

SEASONING AFTER COOKING
- ½ tsp Cumin powder
- 2 tbsp Lemon juice
- 2 tbsp Olive oil
- ½ tsp Sumac (optional)
- 1 pinch Cayenne pepper (optional)
- 1 pinch Salt

METHODE-COOKING

1 Wash and soak the beans overnight in water. Soaking the beans shortens the cooking time and renders them easier to digest.

2 Rinse, drain and sort the beans, removing all the stained beans or the ones with holes.

3 Put the beans in a casserole, add the water, paprika, oil, onion, garlic.
Bring to the boil, turn the heat down completely, cover and allow to cook for 1 hour approximately. Check the cooking and if required add a little hot boiled water and
prolong the cooking time.

4 Add the seasoning at the end of the cooking.

5 Prior to taking off the heat, taste and adjust the seasoning if required.

ADVICE

If you have to add more water, it must be hot boiled water, as the addition of cold water stops the cooking of the pulses. The quantity of water and the cooking time depends on the quality of the beans. We recommend you cook a larger quantity and freeze them in portions.

SUGGESTION

For ease, if short on time, you can purchase tinned ful medammes
and simply heat and season, but it does not compare with the "home made" ones.
It is traditionally served with middle eastern salad, hard boiled egg and tahini sauce.

These beans are available in shops specialising in middle eastern ingredients.

Ful medammes purée
(See recipe Ful Medammes)

METHOD

1 After cooking the ful medammes process it through a vegetable mouli to obtain a bean purée without the skin or put through a food processor then pass through a fine sieve to remove the chopped skin in order to obtain a smooth bean purée.

2 Season with olive oil, lemon juice, salt and a little cumin powder. For quantities see preceding recipe for ful medammes (page 183).

ADVICE

Processing the beans through a vegetable mouli and not a blender enables you to obtain a bean purée without skin which renders the beans more digestible.

This bean purée used to be served to convalescents.

Haricots beans in tomato sauce

PREPARATION 10 MIN COOKING 45 MIN
INGREDIENTS (SERVES 4)
- 200 g Haricots beans (dried)
- 1 Onion, chopped (60 to 70 g)
- 3 tbsp Oil
- 700 ml Water or stock of chicken or meat
- 1 tbsp Tomato purée (concentrate)
- 1 pinch Salt
- 1 pinch Pepper

METHOD

1 Wash and soak the beans overnight.
The soaking shortens the cooking time and renders the beans easier to digest.
2 Rinse, drain and sort the beans, removing any spoiled ones.
3 Put the oil in a casserole, over a medium heat sweat the onion until soft and translucent. Add the beans and the 700 ml of water or stock,
bring to the boil, lower the heat, cover and allow to simmer for 40 min.
approximately. Check the cooking and if required add a little hot
boiled water and cook a while longer.
4 As soon as the beans are cooked, season with the tomato purée,
salt and pepper and allow to boil for a further 5 min.

ADVICE

If you require to add more water, it must be hot boiled water, as the addition
of cold water stops the cooking of the pulses.
The quantity of water and the cooking time depends on the quality of the beans.

SUGGESTION

We always serve the haricots beans with rice, as well as with meat or chicken.
The addition of cereals to pulses turns them into a complete meal.

Haricots beans salad

PREPARATION 10 MIN COOKING 40 MIN
INGREDIENTS (SERVES 4)
- 200 g Haricots beans (dried)
- 700 ml Water
- 1 tbsp Oil

SEASONING
- 2 tbsp Olive oil
- 1 Small bunch of parsley (flat), chopped
- 1 Small onion, chopped or spring onion finely sliced
- 2 tbsp Lemon juice or vinegar (of cider or rice)
- 1 pinch Salt
- 1 pinch Pepper (optional)

METHOD

1 Wash and soak the beans overnight. the soaking shortens
the cooking and renders them easier to digest.

2 Rinse, drain and sort the beans, removing any spoiled ones.

3 Put the haricots beans in a casserole, add the water, bring to the boil.
Cover and allow to cook over a gentle heat for 40 min. approximately.
Check the cooking, if required add a little hot boiled water
and cook a while longer.

4 As soon as the beans are cooked, take off the heat, drain well and allow to cool.
Add the onion, parsley, oil, lemon juice or vinegar, salt and
pepper (optional).
Allow to stand for about 15 minute to enable the seasonings to soak into the
beans and the flavours to develop.

ADVICE

If you require to add more water, it must be hot boiled water,
as the addition of cold water stops the cooking of the pulses.

Loubia

Black eyed bean

PREPARATION 10 MIN COOKING 40 MIN
INGREDIENTS (SERVES 4)
- 200 g Loubia
- 3 Garlic cloves, chopped up
- 2 tbsp Oil
- 500 ml Water or stock of meat or chicken
- 1 pinch Salt
- 1 pinch Pepper

METHOD

1 Wash and soak the loubia overnight.

2 Rinse, drain and sort to remove any spoiled beans.

3 Put the loubia in a casserole with the garlic, the oil, the water and bring to the boil.
Lower the heat, cover and cook over a gentle heat for 40 min.
Check the cooking, if required add a little hot boiled water and cook a while longer.

4 Add the salt and pepper at the end of the cooking.
Taste and adjust the seasoning if required.

ADVICE

If you require to add more water, it must be hot boiled water, as the addition of cold water stops the cooking of the pulses.
The quantity of water and the cooking time depends on the quality of the beans.

SUGGESTION

We always serve the haricots beans with rice, as well as with meat or chicken. The addition of cereals to the pulses turns them into a complete meal.

ORIGINAL RECIPE

The green loubia is a vegetable and like fresh green peas needs podding. The dried loubia is a legume (pulse). Unfortunately, the green variety we used to eat in Egypt is not easily available.

Megadarra
Rice with brown lentils

PREPARATION 15 MIN COOKING 50 MIN
INGREDIENTS (SERVES 4)
- 150 g Rice
- 60 g Lentils brown or green or black beluga (if available)
- 1 Onion, chopped (60 to 70 g)
- 4 tbsp Oil
- 500 ml Water (for the lentils)
- 50 ml Water (for the rice)
- 1 pinch Salt
- 1 pinch Pepper

METHOD

1 Put the oil in a casserole, add the onion and sweat
on a gentle heat until soft and translucent.
2 Add the water, the lentils carefully sorted, washed and drained.
3 Bring to the boil, lower the heat, cover and cook over a gentle heat for 30 min.
approximately. Make sure the lentils are cooked, if necessary add a little hot
boiled water and cook a while longer.
4 Add the 50 ml of water, the salt, the pepper and the washed rice. Mix well,
bring to a gentle boil then simmer covered for a further 20 min.

ADVICE

The black lentils sometime take more time than the brown
or green to cook but tend to maintain their shape in the rice unlike
the brown or green ones that tend to disintegrate.

SUGGESTION

May be served with a Middle Eastern salad (see recipe page 68)
or with (milk or soya) yoghurt.

ORIGINAL RECIPE

Used to be served with fried onions.

Chick Peas casserole

PREPARATION 10 MIN COOKING 50 MIN
INGREDIENTS (SERVES 4)
- 200 g Chick peas
- 1 Onion, chopped (60 to 70 g)
- 3 tbsp Oil
- 500 ml Water or stock of chicken or meat
- 1 pinch Salt
- 1 pinch Pepper

METHOD

1 Wash and soak the chick peas overnight.

2 Drain, rinse and sort the chick peas to remove any impurities.

3 Put the oil in a casserole, add the onion and sweat until soft and translucent.

Add the water or the stock, the chick peas and bring to the boil,

lower the heat, cover and simmer for 50 min. approximately.

4 Check the cooking and if required add some hot boiled water and prolong

the cooking. The salt and pepper should be added at the end of the cooking.

ADVICE

If you require to add more water, it must be hot boiled water,

as the addition of cold water stops the cooking of the pulses.

The quantity of water and the cooking time depends on the quality of the chick peas.

SUGGESTION

As with all pulses, the chick peas are best served with rice, as well as with meat or chicken. With the addition of cereals, the pulses become a complete meal.

In North Africa the chick peas are served with couscous.

Houmous

Chick peas dip

PREPARATION 20 MIN COOKING 40 MIN
INGREDIENTS (SERVES 6-8)
- 150 g Chick peas
- 700 ml Water
- 1 tbsp Oil

SEASONING
- 1 tbsp Tahini paste (sesame seeds paste)
- 2 tbsp Lemon juice
- 2 Garlic cloves, blanched
- 200 ml Water (saved from the chick peas cooking juices)
- 1 bunch Parsley (flat)
- 1 pinch Salt

METHOD

1 Wash and soak the chick peas overnight.

2 Drain, rinse and carefully sort to remove any impurities.

3 Put the oil, water and chick peas in a casserole.
Bring to the boil, lower the heat, cover and simmer for 40 min.

4 Once cooked take off the heat, drain, reserve 200 ml of water from the cooking juice.

5 Blanch the garlic by putting them to boil in 2 tablespoons of water for 2 min.
Remove the garlic cloves, crush them, keep the water and set aside.

6 Place the chick peas in a food processor or blender, add the crushed garlic, the lemon juice, the oil, the tahini paste, the salt and the water from the cooking juice plus the water from the blanched garlic. Blend all the ingredients together until smooth and creamy. Add a little more water if required. Check and adjust the seasoning to your taste.

ADVICE

To lessen the strong taste of raw garlic whilst keeping its flavour,
we recommend you blanch it in boiling water.
The quantity of water and the cooking time depends on the quality of the chick peas.

SUGGGESTION

For ease, if short on time, you can use some tinned chick peas drained and boiled (to soften), then use as directed in the recipe from paragraph 4, however the "home made" ones are still superior.

Split chick Peas
Dahl

PREPARATION 10 MIN COOKING 40 MIN
INGREDIENTS (SERVES 4)
- 200 g Split chick peas
- 1 Onion, chopped (60 to 70 g)
- 4 tbsp Oil
- 500 ml Water or stock of chicken or meat
- 1 pinch Salt
- 1 pinch Pepper

METHOD

1 Wash and soak the split chick peas overnight.

2 Drain, rinse and sort to remove any impurities.

3 Put the oil in a casserole, then over a medium heat sweat the chopped onion until soft and translucent. Add the 500 ml of water or stock with the split chick peas. Bring to the boil uncovered over a gentle heat, wait for the foam to
subside as the water risks spilling over. Turn the heat down, cover and simmer for 40 min. approximately.

4 Check the cooking, if required add some more hot boiled water and prolong the cooking time. At the end of the cooking, add the salt and pepper. Taste and adjust the seasoning if required.

ADVICE

If you require to add more water, it must be hot boiled water, as the addition of cold water stops the cooking of the pulses.

The quantity of water and the cooking time depends on the quality of the chick peas.

SUGGESTION

As with all pulses, the split chick peas are best served with rice. Also can be served with meat or chicken.

With the addition of cereals, the pulses become a complete meal.

In Egypt we consumed rice at almost every meal as an accompaniment to vegetables, meat, chicken, fish and in lemon soups (ham'd).

Rice

White rice

PREPARATION 10 MIN COOKING 30 MIN
INGREDIENTS (SERVES 4-5)
- 200 g White rice
- 50 ml Oil
- 400 ml Water
- 1 pinch Salt

METHOD

1 Put the oil in a casserole, add the rice washed and drained. Stir fry over a gentle heat for 5 to 10 min., stirring all the while to stop it sticking.
2 Add the water and salt, bring gently to the boil, watching it does not over spill, turn the heat down completely, cover and cook for 20 min. Taste and if the rice is not quite cooked, add 3 to 4 tablespoons of water if required and continue cooking until softened.

ADVICE

The stir frying of the rice prior to cooking allows the grains to remain fluffy and separate without sticking.

SUGGESTION

This rice is served as an accompaniment to vegetables, pulses (legumes) and nearly all other main courses.

White rice with vermicelli

PREPARATION 10 MIN COOKING 30 MIN
INGREDIENTS (SERVES 4-5)
- 150 g White rice
- 50 g Vermicelli
- 3 tbsp Oil
- 450 ml Water
- 1 pinch Salt

METHOD

1 Put the oil in a casserole, add the vermicelli
and stir fry over a gentle heat until lightly golden.
2 Add the rice washed and drained, the water, the salt,
mix well and bring gently to the boil, watching it does not spill over.
3 Turn the heat right down, cover and cook for 20 min. approx. until
complete absorbtion of the water.
4 Taste, if the rice is not quite cooked,
add 3 to 4 tablespoons of water and cook a little longer.

ADVICE

The stir frying of the vermicelli, stops it swelling up
and absorbing too much water. It also adds to the taste.

SUGGESTION

This rice is served as an accompaniment to vegetables,
pulses (legumes) and nearly all other main courses.

Brown rice

PREPARATION 10 MIN COOKING 35 MIN
INGREDIENTS (SERVES 4-5)
- 200 g Brown rice
- 3 tbsp Oil
- 500 ml Water
- 1 pinch Salt

METHOD

1 Put the oil, the water and the salt in a casserole, bring gently to the boil.

2 Add the rice washed and drained, cover, turn the heat right down
and cook for 35 min. approximately, until complete absorbtion of the water.

3 Taste, if it is not quite cooked,
add 3 to 4 tablespoons of water and cook a little longer.

ADVICE

To shorten the brown rice's cooking time,
soak the rice for half an hour prior to cooking. The quantity
of water and the cooking time depends on the quality of the rice.

SUGGESTION

This rice is served as an accompaniment to vegetables,
pulses (legumes) and nearly all other main courses.

NOSTALGIC MEMORIES OF FLOWER SCENTED WATERS

During the month of May, when the trees were in bloom,
I remember as a little girl whole days when my mother used to distill
rose petals and orange blossoms into a large glass still
for our yearly supply of scented waters.

Words cannot describe the wonderful "heady" scents and perfumes
that permeated the house for those few days.
What happiness !

When we flavour our pastries with rose or orange flower water,
those unaccustomed to these tastes find these perfumes "exotic"
but for us it is a nostalgic return to our past.

Nowadays when I smell these "heady" perfumes I am taken back
to my country of birth, back to my childhood…
What wonderful memories !

Other than their use in pastries, the flower scented waters were
renowned for their calming, soothing and decongestive properties.

The desserts

*The Konafa / Kataifi can be found in middle eastern, greek, cypriot and ethnic stores. The Filo pastry can also be found in most supermarkets.

Basboussa
Yoghurt and Semolina cake

PREPARATION 25 MIN COOKING / BAKING 35 MIN
INGREDIENTS (12 PIECES)
- 125 g Semolina, medium
- 1 Yoghurt pot (125 ml) or soya yoghurt
- 80 ml Butter (70 g) or mix of 40 ml butter and 40 ml oil
- 30 g Sugar
- 6 g Baking powder
- 100 ml Milk or soya milk
- 12 Blanched almonds for decoration (optional)

SYRUP
- 5 tbsp Honey
- 140 ml Water
- 2 tbsp Orange flower water
- 1 tsp Lemon juice

Ovenproof dish of 14 cm x 19 cm approx. or round of 21 cm in diameter

---

METHOD-SYRUP

Put the honey in a small pan, add the water, the lemon juice and the orange flower water, bring to the boil over a gentle heat, allow to boil for 2 min., take off the heat and set aside.

METHOD-ASSEMBLY

1 Melt the butter.

2 Mix together the semolina, sugar and baking powder. Add the melted butter and mix, add the yoghurt and mix well, then add the milk and thoroughly mix till you obtain a thin batter.
Pour the mix into a well greased ovenproof dish. Allow to stand for 5 min, then place the almonds (if used) at regular intervals over the slightly thickened batter.

3 Place the dish in the preheated oven at 180° C (gas mark 4) for 25 min. When the basboussa is evenly golden remove it. Pour the syrup over and replace into the oven for a further 5 min.

4 Remove from the oven, allow to cool, cut into squares or lozenge shapes.

ORIGINAL RECIPE

Used to be made with butter. The syrup was made with sugar.

Belila

Wheat berries milk pudding

PREPARATION 10 MIN COOKING 50 MIN
INGREDIENTS (SERVES 4)
- 100 g Wheat berries
- 600 ml Water
- 2 tsp Cornflour diluted in 100 ml of milk or soya milk
- 150 ml Milk or soya milk

DECORATION
- 30 g Raisins
- 20 g Nuts (almonds, hazelnuts, pine nuts etc...)
- 20 g Unrefined sugar cane or other
- 1 pinch Cinnamon (optional)

METHOD

1 Wash and soak the wheat overnight.

2 Drain and sort through the wheat carefully and remove any stones or spoiled ones.

3 Put the wheat in a pan with the 600 ml of water, bring to the boil, lower the heat, cover and simmer for 40 min.
Check the cooking, if required add a little hot boiled water and increase the cooking time.

4 As soon as the wheat is cooked, add the milk, the diluted cornflour, the sugar, the raisins and allow to cook for a further 10 min.

5 Serve in glass verrines or ramequins, decorate with chopped nuts and sprinkle with cinnamon (optional).

In Egypt it was customary to serve belila to celebrate a baby's first tooth.
The whole family used to get together and throw a party.

Filo pastry - Assabih Bel Loz

Pastry rolls filled with almonds, pistachios or other nuts

PREPARATION 30 MIN
BAKING 15 MIN
INGREDIENTS (12 PIECES)
- 3 Filo pastry sheets (40 cm x 30 cm)
- 40 ml Oil or butter (melted)
or 20 ml oil 20 ml butter

FILLING
- 30 g Ground almonds
- 30 g Almonds, blanched or pistachios or other nuts, roughly chopped
- 3 tsp Icing sugar
- 2 tbsp Oil or melted butter

SYRUP
- 2 tbsp Honey
- 3 tsp Orange flower water or water

METHOD-FILLING

1 Chop the blanched almonds in a food processor, mix with the ground almonds, sugar and oil. Divide the filling into three equal parts and set aside

METHOD-ASSEMBLY

1 Take a sheet of filo, brush with oil or butter Fig. 1, fold over 10 cm approx. length side and brush with oil Fig. 2.
2 Over the folded part, spread one of the fillings over a 2 cm width stopping at 2 cm from each edge Fig. 3. Fold the side edges of the sheet over the filling and brush with oil Fig. 4, start rolling the sheet with the
filling, squeezing tightly as you roll, carry on rolling in the same manner till you reach the end of the sheet, you should then obtain a roll of 26 cm long approx.
Fig. 5, 6.

3 Place the roll onto a lined baking tray, cut into 4 equal parts without cutting right through Fig. 7. Repeat the same process with the last 2 sheets to form the next 2 rolls. Brush the 3 rolls with oil or butter.
4 Put the tray in a preheated oven at 175 ° C (gas mark 3 ½) for 10 to15 min.
5 While the rolls are baking, prepare the syrup. Put the honey in a small pan with the orange flower water, bring to the boil and boil for 1 min, check it does not boil over. Take off the heat and set aside.
6 Check the cooking of the rolls, remove from the oven as soon as they are nicely golden. Spoon the syrup over immediately. Allow to cool before cutting through and separating the 4 pieces of every roll.

ADVICE

If you are using almonds, blanch them by boiling for 5 min., allow to cool, then slip the skins off.
Our recipe of syrup with honey instead of syrup with sugar is easier and quicker to make.
Whole rolls can be frozen raw ready to bake.

ORIGINAL RECIPE

They used to be made with butter. The syrup used to be made with sugar, lemon juice and water. The whole lot was soaked in too much fat and syrup. In this recipe we have reduced the quantities of fat and replaced the sugar with honey.

The filo pastry is available in supermarkets or ethnic grocers.

Filo pastry – baklava
With almonds, pistachios or other nuts

PREPARATION 50 MIN
COOKING / BAKING 20 MIN
INGREDIENTS (32 PIECES)
- 12 Filo sheets (40 cm x 30 cm approx.)
- 120 ml Oil or butter (melted) or
60 ml oil 60 ml butter

FILLING
- 150 g Ground almonds
- 150 g Almonds, blanched or pistachios or other nuts roughly chopped
- 1 tbsp Icing sugar
- 3 tbsp Oil or butter (melted)

SYRUP
- 5 tbsp Honey
- 3 tbsp Orange flower water or water
- 1 Oven proof dish or tray 28 cm x 20 cm

METHOD-FILLING
1 Chop the almonds in a food processor, put them in a bowl with the ground almonds, the sugar and the 3 tablespoons of oil, mix well and set aside.

METHOD-ASSEMBLY
1 Brush the bottom of the tray with oil.
2 Place half of the sheet of filo in the tray without cutting it, brush with oil, fold over the other half and brush with oil. Brush another 5 sheets in the same manner Fig.1, 2, 3.
3 Put the filling over the sheets of filo, spreading it evenly whilst packing well with the back of a spoon Fig. 4.
4 Cover with the half of another sheet, brush with oil, fold over the other half, brush it with oil and proceed in the same way for the other sheets taking care not to brush the last sheet with oil, as it is easier to cut the baklava before brushing the last one.
5 Cut the baklava in 4 equal parts in the length and 4 equal parts in the width,

you should end up with 16 rectangles of 7.5 cm x 5 cm approx. then cut each rectangle diagonally in two Fig. 5. to form triangles.
6 Using a spoon spread the remainder of the oil carefully over the top of the pastry without disturbing the cut sheets Fig. 6.
7 Place the dish in a preheated oven at 175º C (gas mark 3 ½) for 20 min. approx. till the baklava is nicely golden.
8 While the baklava is baking, prepare the syrup. Put the honey and the orange flower water in a small pan, bring to the boil, boil for 1 min. continually stirring to prevent boiling over. Take off the heat and set aside.
9 Remove the baklava from the oven and immediately spoon the syrup over the top. The lukewarm syrup over the hot baklava, caramelises as it cools.

ADVICE
If you are using chopped almonds, blanch them by boiling in a pan of water for 5 min., allow to cool, then slip the skins off. Our recipe of syrup with honey instead of syrup with sugar is easier and quicker to make. The baklava can keep approx. 2 weeks.
SUGGESTION
You can freeze the baklava in the dish ready to bake.
ORIGINAL RECIPE
It used to be made with butter. The syrup used to be made with sugar, lemon juice and water. The whole lot was soaked in too much fat and syrup. In this recipe we have reduced the quantities of fat and replaced the sugar with honey.

The filo pastry is available in supermarkets or ethnic grocers.

Filo pastry – baklava mignardises
Rolls filled with almonds, pistachios or other nuts

PREPARATION 30 MIN BAKING 15 MIN
INGREDIENTS (20 PIECES)
- 4 Filo pastry sheets (40 cm x 30 cm)
- 40 ml Oil or butter (melted)
or 20 ml oil 20 ml butter

FILLING
- 40 g Ground almonds
- 40 g Almonds, blanched or pistachios
or other nuts roughly chopped
- 3 tsp Icing sugar
- 3 tbsp Oil or butter (melted)

SYRUP
- 2 tbsp Honey
- 3 tsp Orange flower water or water

METHOD-FILLING

1 Chop the blanched almonds in a food processor, place in a bowl and mix with the ground almonds, the sugar, the oil and divide the filling into 2 equal parts and set aside.

METHOD-ASSEMBLY

1 Take a sheet of filo, brush it with oil or butter, place a second sheet over and brush with oil again Fig.1. Fold the 2 sheets together over
10 cm length side and brush the folded part with oil Fig. 2.
2 Over the folded part, spread one of the fillings over a 2 cm width stopping at 2 cm from each edge Fig.3. Fold the sides of the sheets over the filling, brush them with oil Fig.3, 4, roll the sheets squeezing the filling tightly as you roll all the way to the end, you will obtain a roll of 26 cm long approx.
Fig. 5, 6.

3 Place the roll on a lined baking tray, brush with oil, cut it at a slant without cutting right through at regular intervals of 2 cm approx. without separating the baklavas. You will
obtain about 10 pieces Fig.7.
Use the last 2 sheets to make the other roll.
4 Brush the 2 rolls with oil.
5 Put the tray in a preheated oven at 175° C
(gas mark 3 ½) for 15 min. approximately.
6 During the baking of the rolls, prepare the syrup. Put the honey and the orange flower water in a small pan, bring to the boil, boil for 1 min. continually stirring to prevent boiling over. Take off the heat and set aside.
7 Check the baking of the rolls, remove from the oven as soon as they are nicely golden,
spoon the syrup over and detach the pieces off each roll by cutting straight through.

ADVICE

If you are using chopped almonds, blanch them by boiling in a pan of water for 5 min., allow to cool, then slip the skins off. Our recipe of syrup with honey instead of syrup with
sugar is easier and quicker to make. Whole rolls of baklava "mignardises" may be frozen raw ready to bake.

SUGGESTION

These "mignardises" are an easier and more novel way to serve baklava. For an attractive presentation place them in cup cakes.

The filo pastry is available
in supermarkets or ethnic grocers.

Filo pastry- labna and raisins rolls

PREPARATION 30 MIN BAKING 15 MIN
INGREDIENTS (12 PIECES)
- 4 Fillo pastry sheets (40 cm x 30 cm approx.)
- 50 ml Oil or butter (melted) Or 25 ml oil 25 ml butter
- Icing Sugar for sprinkling (optional)

FILLING
- 80 g Labna (see recipe page 52) or cream cheese
- 1 tsp Vanilla sugar
- 30 g Raisins
- 1 tsp Cinnamon (optional)

METHOD-FILLING
Mix all the filling ingredients together in a bowl and set aside.

METHOD-ASSEMBLY
1 Take the 4 sheets of fillo together lengthwise. Cut into 3 equal parts,
giving you 3 strips per sheet of 13 cm x 30 cm approximately Fig.1.
 Place in a plastic bag to prevent them drying.
2 Take a strip with the long side facing you, brush with oil, fold over 10 cm and brush again
with oil Fig. 2. Put a teaspoon of filling at the beginning of the sheet on the folded part up to
2 cm from each end along the width Fig. 3. Fold the sides over 2 cm. Brush the folded sides
with oil Fig.4, roll into a cigar shape to form a roll of 9 cm approximately Fig. 5, 6. Brush the
top with a little oil.
3 Repeat the same process with all the other sheets.
4 Place the rolls on a lined baking tray.
5 Put the tray in a preheated oven at 175°C (gas mark 3 ½) for 10 to 15 min.
6 Check the baking, as soon as the rolls are nicely golden remove
the tray from the oven and allow to cool.
7 Before serving, sprinkle with some icing sugar.

ADVICE
This recipe filled with labna is one of our own adaptation.
For those who are lactose intolerant, we suggest replacing the labna made
with milk by the labna made with soya milk (see recipe page 52).

The filo pastry is available in supermarkets or ethnic grocers.

Aish el-Saraya

Bread of the Royal Palace / bread pudding

PREPARATION 20 MIN
INGREDIENTS (SERVES 4)
- 2 slices Biscottes (light toasted bread available ready made in supermarkets)
- 200 g Crème fraiche or labna (see recipe page 52)
- 40 g Pistachios, shelled, toasted and roughly chopped

SYRUP
- 3 tbsp Honey, runny
- 5 tbsp Orange flower water or rose water

METHOD-SYRUP

Put the honey with the orange flower water in a small pan. Bring to the boil over a gentle heat and boil for 1 min. continually stirring to prevent boiling over.
Take off the heat and set aside.

METHOD-ASSEMBLY

1 Take 4 glass dessert dishes, put half a biscotte roughly broken at the bottom of each.
Pour 1 tablespoon of syrup over the biscotte, spread 50 g of crème fraiche or labna and sprinkle over with the 10 g of chopped pistachios.
Pour another tablespoon of syrup over the crème fraiche and pistachios.
Proceed in the same manner with the other 3 glass dishes.
2 Place in the refrigerator for a few hours.

SUGGESTION

For people intolerant to milk, we suggest you replace
the cream by soya labna (see recipe page 52).

ORIGINAL RECIPE

Used to be made with toasted bread, the syrup was made
with sugar and the cream was full fat cream (Echta).
To obtain the echta we used to have to boil the milk, let it cool,
then skim the surface to retrieve the very thick cream that used to form on top.
In Egypt the echta was bought in specialist dairy shops (crèmeries). It used to be an expensive ingredient (it required several litres of milk for a few grammes of echta).
This dish certainly deserves its title "Bread of the Royal Palace",

Ghorayeba
Middle eastern shortbread

PREPARATION 30 MIN BAKING 10 MIN
INGREDIENTS (15 PIECES)
- 90 g Flour, plain white (fine)
- 25 g Butter
- 40 ml Oil
- 20 g Icing sugar
- 10 g Cornflour
- 2 tsp Orange flower water
- 16 Pistachios or blanched almonds
- 16 Baking cases, 3 cm diameter, 2 cm high (optional)

METHOD

1 Whisk the butter and the sugar in a bowl until it turns white. Add the oil a little at a time. Add the orange flower water, the flour and the cornflour still stirring until it gathers into a well mixed and malleable dough (add a few drops of orange flower water if the dough is not soft enough to work with).

2 Take a piece of dough the size of a walnut of 12 to 13 g approximately, roll into a ball and flatten it slightly to form a ghoraïeba. Proceed in the same manner for the rest of the dough.

3 Once shaped, place the ghoraïebas on a lined oven tray or in baking cases. Place a shelled pistachio or a blanched almond on the top.

4 Bake in a preheated oven at 175°C (gas mark 3 ½) for 8 to 10 min.

Take care not to over bake them as they have to remain white in appearance.

Allow to cool for 10 min before handling as they are fragile when hot.

ADVICE

To obtain ghoraïebas of the same weight and the same size, weigh the dough and divide it by 15. By baking them in the cake cases they are ready to serve.

You can freeze them once cooked or they will keep for about 10 days in an airtight cake tin.

ORIGINAL RECIPE

They were made with butter only and contained more sugar.

Kahk with sugar
Sweet cookie rings with hazelnuts

PREPARATION 45 MIN BAKING 10 MIN
INGREDIENTS (30 PIECES)
- 185 g Flour, plain white (fine)
- 50 ml Oil
- 1 Egg, beaten (set aside 1 tablespoon to eggwash the kahks)
- 45 g Sugar
- 50 g Hazelnuts
- 20 ml Orange flower water or freshly squeezed orange juice
- 2 tsp Baking powder
- 10 g Pistachios or other nuts for decoration (optional)

METHOD

1 Place the hazelnuts in a frying pan and lightly toast them over a medium to low heat, then finely chop and set aside.

2 Beat the egg in a food processor or in a bowl with a hand beater, add the sugar and continue beating until the mixture becomes pale in colour and doubles in volume.
Pour the egg mix into a bowl, add the baking powder, oil, orange flower water (or orange juice), hazelnuts and flour, mix and stir until it all gathers into a malleable dough (add a few drops of orange flower water if the dough is not soft enough to work with).

3 Weigh the dough, divide it into 30 parts. You should obtain parts of 12 g to 13 g approximately, form them into balls Fig. 1. Take a ball and shape it into a baton of 13 cm long approx. Fig. 2, close the baton to form a ring Fig. 3, 4. Proceed in the same manner for the rest of the dough.

4 Place the rings (kahk) on a lined baking tray. With a pastry brush coat the top of the rings with the tablespoon of eggwash (previously set aside) Fig. 5. Where the two ends of the rings meet, decorate with a shelled pistachio. Bake in preheated oven at 175°C (gas mark 3 ½) for 10 min. Check the baking, when the kahks are lightly golden take them out of the oven.

ADVICE

The Kahks can be kept in an airtight cake tin for approximately 1 month.
They can be frozen once cooked.
Without having lost any of their crunchiness the kahks can be eaten
5 minutes after taking out of the freezer.

Khochaf
Dried fruit salad

PREPARATION 30 MIN
INGREDIENTS (SERVES 4)
- 8 Prunes, pitted and washed
- 8 Dates, pitted and washed
- 8 Apricots, washed
- 40 g Raisins, washed
- 12 g Almonds, blanched
- 25 g Pine nuts
- 1 tbsp Orange flower water or rose water
- 250 ml Boiled water

METHOD

Put the thoroughly washed prunes, dates, apricots and raisins in a bowl then add the 250 ml of boiled water, the orange flower or rose water and allow to soak for 5 to 6 hours. Add the almonds and the pine nuts, then share into 4 verrines or ramequins and refrigerate.

Konafa / Kadaifi nests

PREPARATION 40 MIN BAKING 10 MIN
INGREDIENTS (20 PIECES)
- 150 g Konafa
- 60 ml Oil or butter (melted) or 30 ml oil and 30 ml butter

FILLING
- 20 g Ground almonds
- 35 g Pistachios, shelled and roughly chopped or blanched almonds or other nuts
- 2 tsp Icing sugar
- 20 ml Oil or butter (melted) or 10 ml oil and 10 ml butter

SYRUP
- 2 tbsp Honey
- 3 tbsp Orange flower water
- 20 Baking cases for the oven (diameter 3.5 cm x 2 cm high)

METHODE-FILLING
Mix thoroughly in a bowl, the ground almonds, pistachios, sugar and oil, then set aside.

METHOD-ASSEMBLY
1 To enable you to shape the nests, coat the konafa pastry strands with the oil. Take a few   strands of konafa pastry weighing 7 g approx. and 28 cm in length approx. Fig. 1 and roll them round your index finger Fig. 2, 3. Place the shaped nest in a cake case while boring and widening the hole formed to enable you to place the filling into the centre Fig. 4.
2 With the tip of a teaspoon take a little of the filling and keeping the teaspoon in the nest, using your finger slide the filling to the bottom while packing it down Fig. 5. Do not let the filling spill over in order to keep the outside of the pastry tidy and free of nuts Fig.6. Place the filled cases on an oven tray.
3 Put the tray in a preheated oven at 175°C (gas mark 3 ½) for 10 min.
4 While the konafa nests are baking prepare the syrup. Put the honey and the orange flower water in a small pan, bring to the boil over a medium heat and boil for 1 minute, continually stirring in order to stop the syrup spilling over. Take off the heat and set aside.
5 Check the baking, remove the konafa nests as soon as they are a nice golden brown.
Using a teaspoon drizzle a little syrup over the top of the konafa nests Fig. 7.

ADVICE
If the Konafa pastry is dry and you are having problems rolling it around your finger,
add a little more oil to make the strands more malleable.

SUGGESTION You can use these nests with sweet or savoury fillings.
It is a new version of the konafa as "mignardises" (small desserts or petits fours).

The konafa or kadaifi pastry comes raw as a hank of fine pastry, like angel hair or shredded wheat.
It is available in ethnic, Middle Eastern, Greek or Cypriot grocers.

Konafa / Kadaifi in a tray

PREPARATION 30 MIN BAKING 25 MIN
INGREDIENTS (8 PORTIONS)
- 130 g Konafa pastry
- 200 ml Oil or butter (melted) or 100 ml oil and 100 ml butter

FILLING
- 60 g Ground almonds
- 80 g Pistachios, shelled and roughly chopped or blanched almonds or other nuts

SYRUP
- 4 tbsp Honey
- 3 tbsp Orange flower water
- 1 Oven proof dish 19 cm x 14 cm approx.

METHOD-FILLING
Mix together the ground almonds,
the roughly chopped pistachios and set aside.

METHOD-ASSEMBLY
1 Using your hands shred the strands of the whole konafa pastry Fig. 1 and set aside.
2 Put half the konafa pastry in an oven proof dish, add a little oil and pack it down Fig. 2. Put the filling over the pastry, add a little oil and pack it down Fig. 3, 4. Cover with the other half of the pastry and pack it well down Fig. 5. Pour the rest of the oil over the top and pack the finished konafa down Fig. 6.
3 Put in a preheated oven at 180 ºC (gas mark 4) for 20 to 25 min.
4 During the baking, prepare the syrup. Put the honey with the orange flower water in a small pan, bring to the boil over a medium heat and boil for 1 minute, watching that the syrup does not boil over. Take off the heat and set aside.
5 Check on the konafa, as soon as it is golden brown remove from the oven. Drizzle the syrup over the top sharing it evenly over the whole konafa.
6 Once cooled, cut into 8 equal parts.

ADVICE
To finely shred the pastry you can use kitchen scissors. If you are using chopped almonds, skin the raw almonds by boiling them in a pan of water for 5 min., allow to cool, then shell the skins. Our recipe of syrup with honey instead of the syrup with sugar is easier and quicker to make. The tray of konafa may be frozen raw ready to bake

SUGGESTION
We have portioned it into 8 parts
but you can cut it any size you wish.

ORIGINAL RECIPE
It used to be made butter only. The syrup used to be made with sugar, lemon juice and water. The whole konafa was soaked in too much fat and syrup. In this recipe we have reduced the quantities of fat and sugar and replaced the sugar with honey.

The konafa or kadaifi pastry comes raw as a hank of fine pastry like angel hair or shredded wheat. It is available in ethnic, Middle Eastern, Greek or Cypriot grocers.

Konafa / Kadaifi with apples

PREPARATION 15 MIN BAKING 25 MIN
INGREDIENTS (SERVES 4)
- 80 g Konafa pastry
- 100 ml Oil or butter (melted) or 50 ml oil and 50 ml butter
- 3 Apples, 400 g approx.
- 1 tbsp Sugar
- 1 pinch Cinnamon
- 1 tbsp Water
- Cake mould of 21cm in diameter approx.

METHOD-PASTRY CASE

1 Cut and shred the konafa pastry into the cake mould, put the oil or melted butter and pack the konafa pastry well down.
2 Bake in a preaheated oven at 180°C (gas mark 4) for 10 minutes.
Check it is nicely golden before removing from the oven, then set aside.

METHOD-FILLING

1 Put the peeled and quartered apples in a large frying pan with the sugar, cinnamon and water. Cover and cook on a low heat for 10 minutes.
2 Uncover and carry on cooking until complete evaporation of the water. Take off the heat and allow to cool.

METHOD-ASSEMBLY

Lay the apples over the pastry case. See photo.

ADVICE

Best served on the same day while the pastry is still crisp.

SUGGESTION

The pie shell is a new adaptation for the konafa pastry, it can also be served with other sweet or savoury (cheese or other) fillings.
Serve with cream, soya cream or ice cream. The konafa or kadaifi pastry comes raw as a hank of fine pastry like angel hair or shredded wheat.
It is available in ethnic, Middle Eastern, Greek or Cypriot grocers.

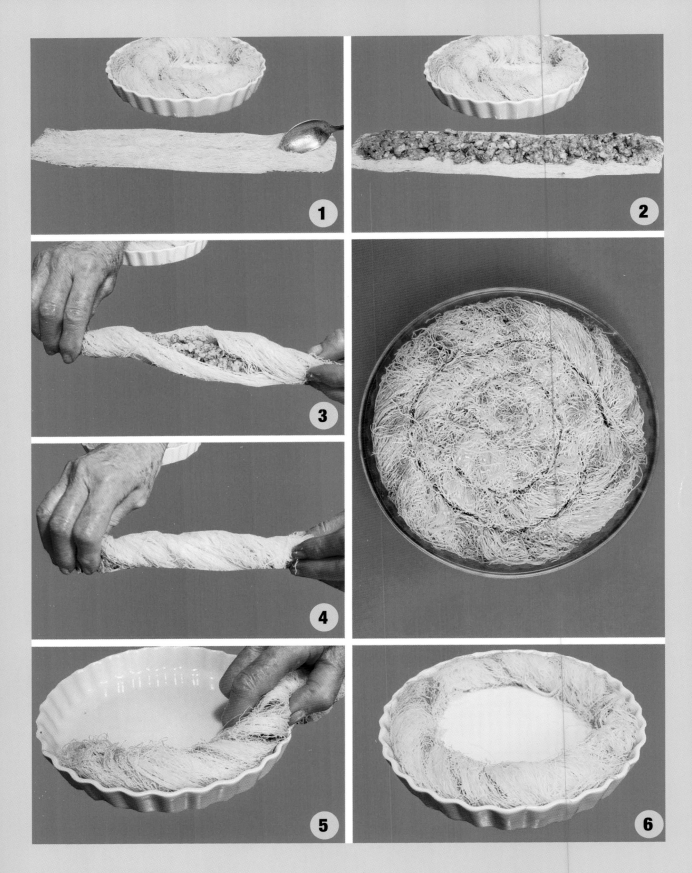

Konafa / Kadaifi roll

PREPARATION 30 MIN BAKING 25 MIN
INGREDIENTS (SERVES 8)
- 180 g Konafa pastry
- 120 ml Oil or butter (melted) or 60 ml oil and 60 ml butter

FILLING
- 140 g Ground almonds
- 175 g Pistachios, shelled or blanched almonds or other nuts roughly chopped
- 1 tbsp Sugar
- 100 ml Oil or butter (melted) or 50 ml oil and 50 ml butter

SYRUP
- 4 tsbp Honey
- 3 tbsp Orange flower water
- Cake mould of 21 cm in diameter approx.

METHOD-FILLING

Mix the ground almonds, pistachios, sugar and oil in a bowl and set aside.

METHOD-ASSEMBLY

1 Detach 45 g of pastry strands, form a strip of 30 cm long by 8 cm wide approx. and coat it with a little oil taken from the 120 ml Fig.1.
2 Over the pastry spread 80 g of filling approx. Fig.2.
3 Turn the 2 ends of the pastry in opposite direction to close it and obtain a roll Fig. 3, 4.
4 Place the roll in the mould while still turning so it remains closed Fig. 5, 6.
5 Proceed in the same manner for the other 3 rolls, taking care to squeeze them tightly against each other. Spoon the remainder of the 120 ml of oil over the konafa pastry rolls.
6 Bake in a preheated oven at 180 °C (gas mark 4) for 20 to 25 min.

7 While the konafa is baking prepare the syrup. Put the honey with the orange flower water in a small pan, bring to the boil over a medium heat and boil for 1 minute, watching that the syrup does not boil over. Take off the heat and set aside.
8 Check the baking, when the top is nicely golden, remove from the oven. Spoon the syrup evenly over the top.
9 Once the konafa has cooled, cut it into any size or shape you wish.

ADVICE

If the Konafa pastry is dry and you are having problems rolling it, add a little more oil to make the strands more malleable.
For this recipe the konafa pastry needs to be very fresh to enable you to turn it easily.
This requires practice, if you still find it hard to roll, make the "Konafa in a tray" (see recipe page 235) which is equally good and easier to achieve.
Our recipe of syrup with honey instead of sugar is easier and quicker to make.
The konafa roll can be frozen raw ready to bake. You will only need to make the syrup to add to the konafa once baked.

ORIGINAL RECIPE

It used to be made with butter only. The syrup used to be made with sugar, lemon juice and water. The whole konafa was soaked in too much fat and syrup. In this recipe we have reduced the quantities of fat and replaced the sugar with honey.
The konafa or kadaifi pastry comes raw as a hank of fine pastry like angel hair or shredded wheat.
It is available in ethnic, Middle Eastern, Greek or Cypriot grocers.

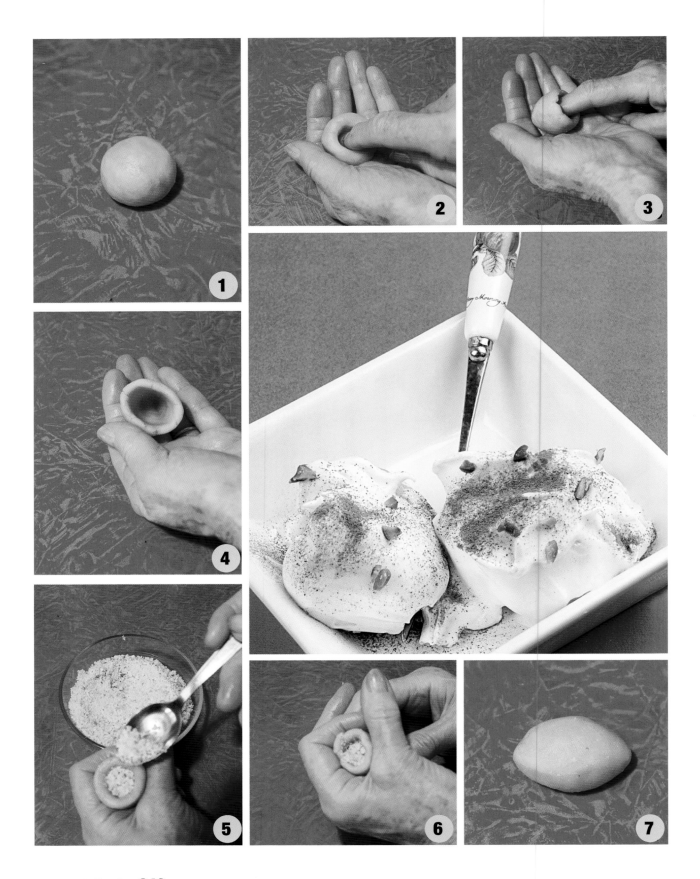

Karabige
Shortcrust pastry filled with almonds

PREPARATION 60 MIN BAKING 15 MIN
INGREDIENTS (15 PIECES)

PASTRY
- 200 g Flour, plain white (fine)
- 1 tsp Baking powder
- 100 ml Oil or butter (melted) or 50 ml oil and 50 ml butter
- 50 ml Orange flower water

FILLING
- 40 g Almonds, blanched or pistachios or other nuts roughly chopped
- 40 g Ground almonds
- 1 tbsp Sugar
- 1 tbsp Oil

METHOD-FILLING
1 Roughly chop the blanched almonds in a food processor, put them in a bowl and mix with the ground almonds, the sugar and the oil then set aside.

METHOD-PASTRY
1 Mix the flour with the baking powder in a bowl, add the oil and amalgamate.
2 Add the orange flower water and bring the flour mix together with your hands, kneading it lightly to form a smooth dough (add a few drops of orange flower water if the dough is not soft enough to work with).

METHOD-ASSEMBLY
1 Shape dough balls the size of a walnut to make 15 pieces of 20 g each approx. Fig.1.
2 Take one ball of dough in the palm of one hand, bore a deep hole in the center with the index finger of the other hand. Widen the hole by turning the dough around your finger to obtain a hollowed out elongated oval shape like an emptied egg shell Fig.2, 3, 4.

3 Using a teaspoon, introduce the filling into the pastry, with the spoon handle pack well down, then close the top of the pastry by gathering the edges together Fig.5, 6.
4 Roll in between the palms of both hands to form an oval shape (a krabige) Fig.7.
5 Proceed in the same manner for the rest of the dough balls. Place the krabiges on a lined baking tray.
6 Bake in a preheated oven 180°C (gas mark4) for 15 min. approx.
Remove from the oven when lightly golden.

ADVICE
If you are using chopped almonds, blanch them by boiling in a pan of water for 5 min, allow to cool, then slip the skins off.
May be frozen raw or cooked.
The krabiges are served with the Natef cream (see recipe page 243).

ORIGINAL RECIPE
The krabiges used to be made with butter only.

Natef for karabige
Honey Cream

PREPARATION 15 MIN COOKING 15 MIN
INGREDIENTS

- 50 ml Honey (runny)
- 1 Egg white
- 5 g Panama bark* (soapworts)
- 150 ml Water
- 1 tsp Cinnamon (optional)
- Pistachios or almonds, chopped for sprinkling (optional)

METHOD

1 To process the panama bark, place it in a pan with the 150 ml of water, bring to the boil uncovered over a gentle heat and allow to reduce to 20 ml approximately. Strain it through a sieve so you are left with the liquid.

2 Whisk the egg white in a mixer for 5 min. until it forms soft peaks.

3 Add the honey and the liquid from the panama bark a little at the time whilst still beating. Just as in a mayonnaise, the egg will emulsify and you will obtain a light whipped white cream. The Natef is served with the krabiges like a whipped cream or chantilly cream, sprinkled with cinnamon. Decorate with roughly chopped pistachios or almonds.

ADVICE

It should be consumed the same day.

If "Panama Bark / soapworts" is unavailable, beat an egg white until soft peaks form, add the honey a little at a time while still beating until you obtain firm peaks as you would for a meringue mix.

* Panama bark / soapworts can be bought in herbalist shops.

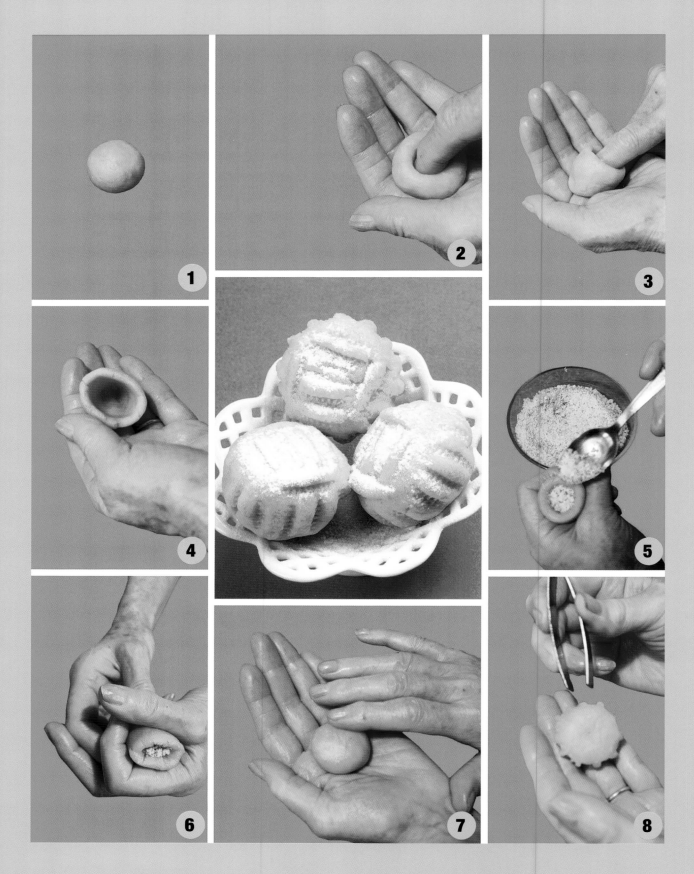

Ma'amoul / Menena
with almonds / pistachios / walnuts
Shortcrust pastry filled with nuts

PREPARATION 60 MIN
BAKING 15 MIN
INGREDIENTS (15 PIECES)

PASTRY
- 200 g Flour, plain white (fine)
- 1 tsp Baking powder
- 100 ml Oil or butter (melted) or 50 ml oil and 50 ml butter
- 50 ml Orange flower water

FILLING
- 40 g Almonds, blanched or pistachios or other nuts roughly chopped
- 40 g Ground almonds
- 1 tbsp Sugar
- 1 tbsp Oil
- 1 tbsp Icing sugar (for sprinkling)

METHOD-FILLING

1 Roughly chop the blanched almonds, put them in a bowl and mix with the ground almonds, the sugar and the oil then set aside.

METHOD-PASTRY

1 Mix the flour with the baking powder in a bowl, add the oil and amalgamate.
2 Add the orange flower water and bring the flour mix together with your hands, kneading it slightly to form a smooth dough (add a few drops of orange flower water if the dough is not soft enough).

METHOD-ASSEMBLY

1 Shape balls of dough the size of a walnut to make 15 pieces of 20 g each approx. Fig.1.
2 Place a ball of dough in the palm of one hand and bore a deep hole in the center with the index finger of the other hand. Widen the hole by turning the dough to obtain a hollowed out elongated oval shape Fig.2, 3, 4.
3 Using a teaspoon introduce the filling into the pastry. Pack well down with the spoon handle, close the top of the pastry by gathering the edges together Fig.5, 6.
4 Roll the filled dough in between the palms of both hands to reshape it into a ball Fig.7.
5 Flatten the ball slightly, then with pastry tweezers pinch the dough at regular intervals, first around the ball Fig.8, then on the top to enable the icing sugar to adhere to the pastry.
6 Proceed in the same manner with the rest of the dough and place the ma'amouls on a lined baking tray.
7 Bake in a preheated oven at 180ºC (gas mark 4) for 10 to 15 min. Remove from the oven when they are lightly golden. Allow to cool before sprinkling the icing sugar.

ADVICE

If you are using almonds, blanch them by boiling for 5 min., allow to cool, then slip the skins off.
Can be frozen raw or cooked.
Can be served in individual baking cases.
ORIGINAL RECIPE
The ma'amouls used to be made only with butter.

Ma'amoul / Menena with dates

Shortcrust pastry rolls filled with dates

**PREPARATION 60 MIN BAKING 15 MIN
INGREDIENTS (20 PIECES)**

PASTRY
- 130 g Flour, plain white (fine)
- 1 tsp Baking powder
- 60 ml Oil or butter OR 30 ml oil 30 ml butter
- 30 ml Orange flower water

FILLING
- 80 g Dates, pitted and minced or date paste
- 6 g Clementine or tangerine peel,
minced (organic if possible)
- 1 tbsp Oil
- 3 tbsp Water
- 1 tbsp Icing sugar (for sprinkling)

METHOD-FILLING

1 In a bowl mix the minced dates with the minced clementine peel.

2 Place the mixture in a frying pan over a low heat with 1 tablespoon of oil and the 3 tablespoons of water. Mash with a fork for 5 to 10 min. to render the mix malleable and to enable you to spread it easily. Take off the heat, allow to cool slightly, then separate the mix into 2 equal parts and set aside.

METHOD-PASTRY

1 In a bowl mix the flour with the baking powder, add the oil and amalgamate.

2 Add the orange flower water and bring
 the flour mix together with your hands, kneading it slightly to form a smooth dough
(add a few drops of orange flower water
if the dough is not soft enough).

3 Divide the dough into 2 equal parts and set aside.

METHOD-ASSEMBLY

1 Shape one part of the dough into a sausage Fig.1, then flatten with a rolling pin to shape into a rectangle of 25 cm x 10 cm Fig.2.
Using the back of a spoon flatten one part of the filling over the dough stopping 1 cm from the edges Fig.3.

2 From the long edge nearest to you, start rolling the pastry over the filling to obtain a roll of 4 cm in diameter approx. by 25 cm long, Fig. 4, 5, flatten the roll slightly, close the two ends diagonally, then cut diagonally at regular intervals of 2,5 cm approx., so you obtain 10 pieces of ma'amoul Fig. 6.

3 Detach the ma'amouls and pinch the tops with pastry tweezers or by hand to enable the icing sugar to adhere to the pastry Fig. 7.

4 Proceed in the same manner with the second part of pastry. Put the ma'amouls on a lined baking tray.

5 Place the tray in a preheated oven at 180°C (gas mark 4) for 10 to 15 min.
Take them out of the oven when they are lightly golden. Allow to cool before sprinkling the icing sugar (optional).

ADVICE

To spread the dough easily without it sticking and for ease of handling, take a sheet of greaseproof paper 30 cm x 30 cm, fold it in two, put the roll of dough inside and flatten with a rolling pin Fig.2.
Make use of the greaseproof paper to enable you to lift and roll the pastry easily Fig.4.

SUGGESTIONS

Can be frozen raw or cooked.
Can be served in individual baking cases.
The clementine peel can be frozen so it can be used out of season.

ORIGINAL RECIPE

The ma'amouls used to only be made with butter.

Mehalabeya
Cornflour milk pudding

PREPARATION 15 MIN COOKING 10 MIN
INGREDIENTS (SERVES 4)
- 400 ml Milk or soya milk
- 25 g Cornflour
- 2 tbsp sugar
- 80 ml Water
- 1 tbsp Orange flower water or rose water
- 1tsp mastic with sugar (optional)
- 20 g Pistachios or blanched almonds roughly chopped for decoration
- 1 pinch Cinnamon (optional)

METHOD

1 Dilute the cornflour in the 80 ml of water.

2 If used dilute the mastic with sugar in 20 ml of water taken from the 80 ml.

3 Put the milk or soya milk in a pan, add the diluted cornflour, the orange flower water, the sugar, the diluted mastic with sugar and bring to the boil over a medium heat while stirring.

4 As soon as the liquid thickens turn off the heat and pour into 4 verrines or ramequins.

5 Decorate with the roughly chopped pistachios or almonds or any other nuts, sprinkle with cinnamon if desired.

MASTIC FLAVOURED SUGAR

(Our own original recipe)

To enable the mastic to be utilised in desserts it has to be mixed with sugar so as to stop it coagulating.

Pulverise 3 g of mastic in a coffee mill with 30 g of sugar to make powdered sugar with mastic flavour ready to use. One teaspoon of the mix is a good quantity to flavour 500 ml to 1 litre of liquid. It must always be diluted in 2 tablespoons of cold water prior to use.

The mastic is very aromatic, it is used in very small doses in oriental desserts, such as turkish delights and ice creams.

As with the flower scented waters, mastic gives an exotic flavour typical of the Middle East. It is best kept in a sealed jar.

Mastic is available in ethnic or Middle Eastern, Greek or Cypriot grocers.

ORIGINAL RECIPE

Mehalabeya only used to be made with milk.

Pâte d'amandes

Almond sweatmeats / Marzipan

**PREPARATION 20 MIN
COOKING 20 MIN
INGREDIENTS (10 PIECES)**
- 75 g Ground almonds
- 30 g Icing sugar
- 1 tsp Orange flower water
or rose water (optional)
- 70 ml Water or colorant
- 10 Pine nuts, pistachios (shelled)
or any other nuts for decoration
- 10 Baking cases 3 cm
in diameter and 2 cm deep approx.

NATURAL COLORANTS
- Yellow: 30 g mango or orange
plus a pinch of turmeric
- Rose : 30 g raspberries
or strawberries, fresh or frozen
- Red : 30 g raw beetroot
- Green : 30 g raw spinach or parsley

METHOD-COLORANT

Yellow: mix 30 g of mango or orange pulpe with
a pinch of turmeric, strain through a fine sieve to
retrieve the juice only, add a little water if required
so you can obtain 70 ml of liquid.
Rose : with a fork mash 30 g of strawberries or
raspberries, strain through a fine sieve to retrieve
the juice only, add a little water if required so you
can obtain 70 ml of liquid.
Red: finely grate 30 g approx. of raw beetroot,
strain through a fine sieve to retrieve the juice only,
add a little water if required to obtain 70 ml of
liquid.
Green : in a mixer or blender reduce to a pulp 30
g of parsley or raw spinach with two tablespoons
of water, strain through a fine sieve to retrieve the
juice only, add a little more water if required to
obtain 70 ml of liquid.

These natural colorants give the colours without
having to use artificial colorants.

METHOD-PÂTE D'AMANDES

1 Put the ground almond, the sugar, the water
in a frying pan over a low heat. Add the colorant
of your choice, the orange flower water and
stir continuously for 5 to 10 min. until complete
evaporation of the water. Allow to cool.
2 Oil your hands and roll the mix into 10 balls of
14 g approximately, flatten them slightly, place
them in the baking cases and decorate with pine
nuts or pistachios in the center.
3 Bake in a preheated oven at 180°C (gas mark 4)
for 10 min. approximately.

ADVICE

These almond sweetmeats (marzipan) keep for 4
to 5 days in an airtight box or a few months in the
freezer. We recommend you produce this quantity
per colour. You can also obtain other colours with
blueberries, carrots etc.

Roz bel Laban

Middle eastern rice pudding

PREPARATION 15 MIN COOKING 25 MIN
INGREDIENTS (SERVES 4)
- 500 ml Milk or soya milk
- 40 g Round rice
- 1 tbsp Orange flower water or rose water
- 1tsp mastic with sugar diluted in 2 tbsp of water, see recipe page 249 (optional)
- 2 tbsp Sugar
- 1 pinch Cinnamon (optional)
- A few raisins, blanched almonds, pine nuts, pistachios, etc. for decoration

METHOD

1 Put the milk in a pan, add the washed and drained rice, bring to the boil uncovered over a gentle heat. Lower the heat and simmer for 20 min. approx. Stir frequently, checking the rice is not sticking to the bottom of the pan.

2 Towards the end of the cooking, add the sugar, the diluted sugar with mastic (if used) and the orange flower water (or rose water).
Allow to boil gently for a further 5 min.

3 Pour into 4 verrines or ramequins. Decorate with raisins, almonds, pine nuts, pistachios and sprinkle with cinnamon (optional).

ADVICE

May be served hot or cold. It keeps 5 to 6 days under refrigeration.
To stop the rice spilling over, cook uncovered in a larger pan.

Date Rolls

Petits fours of dates and nuts

PREPARATION 45 MIN COOKING 25 MIN
INGREDIENTS (2 ROLLS)
- 250 g Dates pitted
and minced
- 60 g Pecan nuts
- 30 g Almonds, blanched
- 30 g Hazelnuts
- 60 g Pistachios, shelled
- 40 g Sesame seeds
- 2 tbsp Oil
- 120 ml Water

METHOD

1 In a frying pan, lightly toast separately, the pecan nuts, blanched almonds, hazelnuts, pistachios and sesame seeds. Allow to cool, then roughly chop all the nuts except the sesame seeds and set aside.

2 Put the minced dates in a frying pan, add the water and oil. Cook over a gentle heat while you mix and stir until you obtain a well homogenised paste.

3 Add the pecan nuts, almonds, hazelnuts pistachios and amalgamate.
Take off the heat and allow to cool.

4 Divide the paste into 2 equal parts, take one part and roll it in a long roll of 3.5 cm in diameter and 28 cm long approximately, then roll in the toasted sesame seeds.
Proceed in the same manner for the second roll.

5 Place in the refrigerator for a few hours.
Cut the rolls into even slices.

ADVICE

May be frozen in whole rolls.
Keeps well in an airtight box.
The nuts are lightly toasted to crisp them up and enhance their flavour.

SUGGESTION

Can be served in individual cake cases.

DRIED FRUITS AND NUTS

Fruits in the Middle East used to be eaten in season.
Out of season, due to the difficulty of conservation (refrigeration and freezing),
they were replaced by dried fruits.

The dried fruits such as raisins, apricots, prunes, figs etc.
and the nuts such as almonds, hazelnuts, walnuts, cashew nuts,
pecan nuts, pine nuts, pistachios, etc. are plentiful in the Mediterranean
and Middle Eastern countries. They often enhance many
dishes, desserts and pastries.

All these dried fruits and nuts are an important source
of vitamins, minerals and fibre.
They are high in calories. Don't deprive yourself but don't overindulge.

VEGETABLES AND FRUITS

Every vegetable and every fruit contains its own specific vitamins
and nutrients in varying degrees, such as vitamin c, magnesium, potassium, beta
carotene etc.
The same principle applies to all vegetables and fruits, as full of vitamins as each one of
them is, none of them singly is a panacea. For that reason, it is recommended to consume
several varieties daily.
Eat the vegetables and fruits when in season and as fresh as possible.
The vegetables and fruits that have spoiled are devoid of any vitamins.

Useful advice

Vegetables and Fruits : If possible use Organic when available but they must always be extremely fresh. It is the freshness that will give the best flavours to the cooking. You can only produce good food with very good produce.

Washing products for vegetables and fruits :
Organic washing up liquid, bicarbonate of soda, vinegar.
Organic washing up liquid: Tomatoes, cucumbers, lettuces, herbs etc.
Bicarbonate of soda: Strawberries, blueberries etc.
Vinegar: Broccolis, cauliflowers etc.
Always rinse well before use.

CONSERVATION UNDER REFRIGERATION

The Herbs : dill, mint, parsley, coriander, etc. Organic if possible.
When buying the herbs they must not be yellowing and lifeless. They must always appear to be freshly cut and bright green.
Put a drop of soap in the rinsing water, wash it well off, rinsing in clear water, in a salad spinner spin the water off and place them in lidded glass containers (oven and freezer containers) lined with two plies of absorbent kitchen paper. Put your herbs in without squashing them, cover with another sheet of absorbent kitchen paper and cover with the lid. You will have fresh herbs for 5 to 7 days.

Cucumbers : Organic if possible, buy it rigid and very green. Wash it, dry it, wrap it in absorbent kitchen paper, then in a plastic bag, it will keep fresh for a good few days.

Vegetables for cooking : If they are not to be used on the same day of purchase, do not wash them but wrap them in absorbent kitchen paper, then slip them in plastic bags, they will keep fresh a few days.

Fruits : Tomatoes, lemons, apples, oranges etc.
place them under refrigeration in the vegetables and fruit drawer..

Advice

Use the very practical and useful special glass containers (freezer to oven)
of different sizes for all cooked food.
Avoid the use of plastic containers as they can alter the flavours
and are more difficult to degrease.
Never put in your fridge any food such as cheese, butter and left overs without cover.

Cooking

Cooking : Always with gentle moderate heat.
Quick-braising in its own juice (a l'etuvee), or steamed,
occasionally in the oven or fried.

Casserole : Use preferably glass, enamelled and stainless steel casseroles.
Select pans with glass lids, you will be able to check the food
while it simmers without lifting the lid.

Advice : After all meals, empty immediately all the left
overs into containers, cover and refrigerate.

A

B

C

Conversion charts

Weights

UK /US	METRIC
1/4 oz	7 g
1/2 oz	15 g
1 oz	30 g
2 oz	55 g
3 oz	85 g
4 oz	110 g
5 oz	140 g
6 oz	170 g
7 oz	200 g
8 oz	225 g
9 oz	250 g
10 oz	280 g
11 oz	310 g
12 oz	340 g
13 oz	370 g
14 oz	400 g
15 oz	425 g
16 oz (1 lb.)	450 g

Volume

IMPERIAL	AMERICAN	METRIC
	$1^{1/4}$ tsp	1.25 ml
	$1^{1/2}$ tsp	2.5 ml
	1 tsp	5 ml
	$1^{1/2}$ tbsp	7.5 ml
	1 tbsp	15 ml
2 fl oz	$1^{1/4}$ cup	60 ml
2 1/2 fl oz	1/3 cup	75 ml
4 fl oz	$1^{1/2}$ cup	125 ml
5 fl oz	2/3 cup	150 ml
6 fl oz	3/4 cup	175 ml
8 fl oz	1 cup	250 ml
10 fl oz	$1^{1/4}$ cup	300 ml
12 fl oz	$1^{1/2}$ cup	350 ml
16 fl oz	1pint (2cups)	500 ml
20fl oz (1pint)	$2^{1/2}$ cups	625 ml
40fl oz (1qt)	5 cups	1.25l

*Oven temperatures

	*F	*C	GAS MARK
Very cool	250-275	130-140	1/2 -1
Cool	300	150	2
Warm	325	165	3
Moderate	350	175-180	3 1/2 - 4
Moderately hot	375-400	190-205	5-6
Hot	425	220	7
Very hot	450-475	230-245	8-9

*The oven temperatures have been rounded off

Glossary of Terms
British and American Terms

UK	US
Plain flour	All purpose flour
Strong flour	Unbleached white flour
Cornflour	Cornstarch
Coriander	Cilantro
Semolina	Cream of wheat
Icing sugar	Confectioners' sugar
Bicarbonate of soda	Baking soda
Hazelnuts	Filberts
Vanilla essence	Vanilla extract
Whipped cream	Heavy cream
Aubergines	Eggplants
Courgettes	Zucchini
Petit Pois	Spring peas
Spring onions	Green onions/Scallions
Minced meat (beef, veal, lamb)	Ground meat (beef, veal, lamb)
Baking tray	Cookie sheet
Frying pan	Skillet
To grill	To broil
The grill	The broiler
Greaseproof paper	Vegetable parchment

Published by M&N Publishing Limited
Griffin Court 201 Chapel Street Manchester M3 5EQ United Kingdom - Company number 8910957
Nelly Sultan and Nina Mellman have asserted their rights to be identified as authors of this work in accordance with the Copyright, Designs and Patents Act 1988.
Copyright © Nelly Sultan & Nina Mellman November 2014
Cataloguing in Publication Data is available from the British Library
ISBN 978-2-9547636-0-6
Photography Nelly Sultan & Nina Mellman
Printed by Burelor, Argenteuil, France
Website : www. middleeasterncookery.com